The Chinese Purse

Loretta H. Wang

 HILIT PUBLISHING CO., LTD.

Second Edition Mar. 31, 1991
All Worldwide Rights Reserved
All objects illustrated are from the
collection of the author except where
noted. No reproduction of these designs
is permitted.

Author and Editor: Loretta H. Wang
Photographers: J. Chen and K. Lin
Designer: Gary Wang

This book is published simultaneously in
Chinese and English.

Copyright under Highlight International.

Printed and bound in Taiwan.

ABOUT THE AUTHOR

Loretta Hui-Lang Wang was born in Taiwan
and studied Chinese literature in Taiwan
University, Taipei, Taiwan. She studied textile
design in the Fashion Institute of Technology,
New York, and became a textile designer. She
and her husband now have their own design
firm, Wang Designs, located in the fashion
center of Manhattan.

COVER PHOTOS

The front and back cover photos depict two
sides of an imperial purse of the *Ch'ing*
Dynasty.
The purse has two different colored sides.
One side of the purse is cream and the other
side is yellow. It is decorated with peonies,
the phoenix, and pheasants.

Preface

When I was a little girl in China, my grandmother would draw a butterfly or a flower on a piece of paper, and my sisters and I would fill in the colors. Years passed, those beautiful patterns and colors continued to fascinate me. It was only natural that I should become a textile designer. Now I live and work with colors, patterns, and shapes; my favorite childhood pasttime has become my career. My husband and I have collected, over the years, antique textile pieces and we have grown to love Chinese embroidered pieces. Of our entire textile collection, we favor our treasured group of purses. Their daintiness, brilliant colors, intricate embroidery, and variety of shapes make them more unique than other categories of Chinese embroidery.

Beautiful as they are, these purses have been forgotten in today's world. Few people have any knowledge of their use, how they were created, and there are very few articles written on this special art. This is particularly sad as it was only eighty years ago, in our grandparents' time, that purse-making was a thriving and popular art. Every Chinese girl was taught to embroider at a young age, the purse as her first important project. When her skill was refined, as an adolescent, she would secretly make a special purse for her beloved. As a wife, she would create purses for her in-laws as traditional gifts from the bride. Almost all Chinese women of this era spent their days and nights embroidering. The woman remained anonymous yet the work she left behind is so beautiful and unique that it is still treasured.

A variety of purses are shown in this book, made by housewives as well as skilled masters, some extremely elaborate and fanciful, others naive and simple. The purpose of this book is to present this art form with regard to the way it was practiced; it was both a popular handicraft and a great art worth devoting one's life to.

Women's social status has changed drastically in the China of today. Women are no longer seen hunched over their embroidery frames. These purses are not only beautiful and nostalgic, but represent the last era in Chinese old world history. The last romantic, peaceful, slow, and terribly dated period of Chinese history. I wonder if this art form could be brought back to life, but perhaps in a different way.

When I started collecting these purses I showed them to my grandmother and mother-in-law for their advice. As women born in the transitional period between the old and new China both were still familiar with the purses and very enthusiastic about this book. Today, both of these women are gone. Like the countless women before them who have left us the memories of joy, color, and love, I dedicate this book to them.

Peddler is Selling Purses
A City of Cathay (Detail)
Joint work by Sun Hu, Chin K'un, Tai Hung, Ch'en Chih-tao and Ch'en Mei. Ch'ing Dynasty.

CONTENTS

Horsemen with Purses
Hundred Horses and Grooms (Detail)
Lang Shih-ning or Giuseppe Castiglione, Ch'ing Dynasty.

The Story of Embroidered Purses

For most of the Chinese people, "purse" is an expression associated with romantic gifts of honor and love. In old Chinese novels and dramas, a purse could be a packet filled with precious jewels that was used as a dowry for a daughter from a rich family, or an embroidered wallet tenderly made by a young maiden in her chamber to be secretly given to her beloved one. In 1911, when the *Ch'ing* (清) Dynasty ruling class was cast off by a revolution and replaced with a democratic system, the old customs were also cast aside. These purses lost their meaning in this new modern society. Impractical and dated customs were replaced with new personal freedom in attire.

Among all of the world's cultures, only the Chinese and the Scots were known to have worn bags at their waist. (The Scots wore bags in their daily attire, but only when dressing in kilts). Some historians have suggested that these Chinese purses were only worn with the traditional Chinese costume because the robe did not have pockets. This theory is not necessarily true; many of the traditional robes did have inside pockets attached to the lining and jackets of the late Ch'ing period had exposed pockets.

These purses were the staple accessory for the fashionable man. He might have worn as many as ten on his waist at one time. They were status symbols; representations of a man's wealth and importance in society. Their practical use was outweighed by social significance.

The Origin of Waist Hangings

Waist hangings originated with pre-historic man. *Peking Man*, who inhabited China over five hundred thousand years ago, used string to carry his tools on his waist.

Belts of the In-Shang (殷商) period

The earliest historical documents, describing different kinds of social systems and rules, can be traced back to the *Shang* (商) Dynasty (1766–1121 B.C.). According to the law of the time, people were divided into several classes; kings, civilians, slaves, etc. Important citizens enjoyed the custom of wearing a belt around the waist to indicate the individual's rank in the class structure.

Jade miniatures that were found at *An-Yang In Tombs* (安陽殷墓) show the shapes of these strips. They were in the shape of an ax; narrow at the top and wide at the bottom. The Chinese name for these strips is *"Bi"* (鞸). Bi were made of leather and painted with colors. Strips made of embroidered silk were called *"Fu"* (黻). *(see figure 1)*

This period marked the beginning of waist hangings as status symbols with different colors, textures, and patterns representing rank in the social hierarchy. The strips on an emperor's belt would be embroidered orange, a prince wore embroidered red, and the higher rank officials wore green. Embroidered red strips were bestowed by emperors as a reward for great merit.

Fig. 1

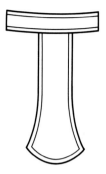

Waist Hangings of the Chou Dynasty

The emperor's advisor, *Chou-Kung*, (周公) of the *Chou* (周) dynasty (1121-225 B.C.) instituted rules for the use of costume appendages in his law-making. Sculpted jade charms were a new addition to the belts.

Government officials wore two belts; one leather band worn under a larger silk band. The silk band was held in place by a large decorative bow. *(see figure 2)*

Fig. 2

The leather belt served a practical function for the gentleman. Long swords, jade ornaments, sachets, packets, ancient writing knives, and writing palettes were tucked under the strong leather band. The writing palette was made of ivory, jade, or bamboo stem wrapped in sharkskin. The official carried this palette with him when he convened with the emperor. With a brush pen, he wrote his thoughts on this palette. When not in use, the palette was re-attached to his leather belt. *(see figure 3)*

Fig. 3

The Chinese word of the *Chou* Dynasty meaning "Belt-man" has evolved to mean "gentleman" in today's language, one indication of the great prestige associated with the wearing of the silk band.

The robe was the standard attire for both men and women for all occasions. The only variations came in the width of the sleeves and the length of the robe. In the latter part of the *Chou* Dynasty, the Warring-States period, the first change of dress emerged. In 320 B.C., *Chao-Wu-Ling,* (趙武靈) King of *Chao,* (趙) adopted the western Nomads' clothing for his warrior's fighting costume. The short, fitted top and riding pants proved to be more convenient for strenuous activity, (ie., hunting, working, and riding horses). The belt buckle *(see figure 4)* was introduced to the Chinese as the focus of this costume. The buckle was slender and one end was narrow for fastening. The buckles were made of brass with gold, silver and jade inlay, or sculpted jade or ivory. This belt still served the same practical function as before. A new, respected craft emerged in central China; the belt buckle became a new status symbol to be replaced later, in the *East Han* (東漢) period, by the "Silver Nine-Rings belt".

Fig. 4

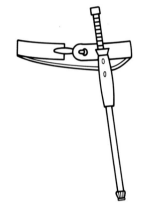

Waist Hangings in the Han Dynasty (Signet, Sash bags, and Amulets)

The official's dress, cap, and waist hangings of the *Han Dynasty* were made specifically according to social status and rank. As in earlier history, two belts were worn; one for identification and one for function. The narrower, functional belt was called a *"Ju"* (組) and the larger, wider belt was the *"Shou"* (綬). Both were made of silk. The *Ju* remained a man's belt for practical use, the *Shou* was awarded to an officer by the court he served. The length of the *Shou*, the color, and the number of pendants indicated the man's rank in his emperor's court. An official seal was also awarded to the officer, (a medal of rank), and attached at the end of the *Shou*, beneath a bow, on his right hip. A leather bag, *"Sash Bag"*, was worn next to the sash and used to store the precious seal from loss. This leather bag was decorated with a painted motif. The *Shou* was much wider than before; up to six inches in width, and five to fifteen feet in length. The highest officials had the longest *Shous*. Up to four colors were used in the woven patterns of the decorative sashes *(see figure 5)*. "Gung-Mao" (岡功) was attached to the narrow belt. *Gung-Mao* were two pieces of carved metal or jade worn as personal protection against evil spirits. These two ornaments were worn for personal reasons. This amulet was made on the fourth *(Mao)* day of January and with special wordings carved on all four sides of each square amulet. An emperor's *Gung-Mao* was carved out of white jade, and high-ranking officials often used rhinoceros horn or ivory.

Fig. 5

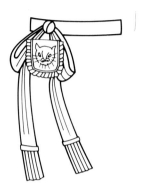

The Nine-Rings Belt of the Wei-Chin (魏晉) Dynasty:

The Nine-Rings belt, its name derived from the original Nomadic pronounciation, was also called the *Dei-Hsieh* (蹀躞) belt. This belt was a leather belt with nine decorative inlays and small hanging strips. *(see figure 6)*

Fig. 6

Because of the assimilation of the Nomads with the *Han*, (Northern Nomads migrated to Central China fleeing wars and famine), common attire underwent some changes, and the Han people adopted the narrower sleeves, fitted top, and *Dei-Hsieh* belt and boots of the Nomads.

The Dei-Hsieh Belt and Fish Bag of the Early T'ang Dynasty:

The leather belt of the Northern Nomads had become popular among the people of Central China in the early *T'ang* (唐) period. By 674 A.D., the Nomads' leather belt had become a part of every official's formal attire. Later in the *T'ang* period, officials were commanded to return to the traditional silk Big Band but the *Dei-Hsieh* belt remained fashionable among the civilian population and particularly among the women. The *Dei-Hsieh* belt was kept for its practical usage. Fire stone, needles, knives, flint and tinder sets, and other necessities, (called the "seven necessities"), hung from the *Dei-Hsieh* belt and afforded the wearer with easy access to the tools of everyday living.

In subsequent years, court maidens wore the narrow leather belt with hanging carved or inlay decorative strips, replacing the "seven necessities". *(see figure 7)*

Fig. 7

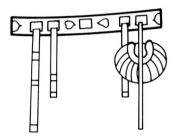

In the *T'ang* and *Sung* (宋) Dynasties, court officials wore the Big Band as a loose, wide leather belt. The Big Band belt was still a part of an official's costume and a means of distinguishing his rank. This leather belt, now called a *"Cheng"* (鞓), was decorated with semiprecious inlay in rectangular or round shapes called *"Kua"* (銙). Jade, gold, silver, brass, rhinoceros horn, stone, and black jade were carved into *Kuas*. The decorated side was turned to the back of the waist so that it was not obscured by the wearer's hands or sleeves. The *Cheng* was secured by buckles on sides of the waist. Construction of the buckles was similar to modern buckles and decorated on the left end of the front piece. A variation of this belt is worn in the costumes of the *Peiking* opera of today. *(see figure 8)*

Fig. 8

During the early *T'ang* period, a "fish label" (or badge) was worn by the court officials. This gold, silver, or brass badge was a three inch long fish shape split into twin sections. The incised wordings on the badge identified its owner. The wearer retained one section as his identification upon entrance to court, while the second part was left at the office of central government. A "fish label bag", a small fabric pouch, was used as a container for this badge. The bag was named after Emperor Li, the ruler of the period, whose name was homonymous with "carp", thus the name "fish" bag. The open eyes of the fish symbolized the strength of the *Li-Tang* Dynasty. Both the fish bag and the fish badge were bestowed upon the officer as medals of honor by his court. *(see figure 9)*

Fig. 9

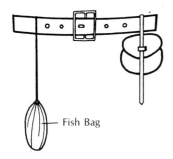

— Fish Bag

During the Five Dynasties (五代) and the *Sung* Dynasty, the fish badge evolved into a simpler shape. Now a curved strip hung on a red leather belt, it was decorated with gold and silver fish patterns. These patterns were entirely different from those inscribed on the earlier fish badge. The badge and bag were worn only by officials of the higher ranks.

In the northern region, kings kept the *Dei-Hsieh* belt as gifts for their trusted followers. The belt was kept in use by the Nomads of that area.

In the *Southern Sung* (南宋) period, the *Liao* (遼) people of the north decreed that the *Han* officials keep the seven necessities of the *Dei-Hsieh* on their waist with traditional costume still permitted among the common population.

The Seven Necessities of the Yuan and Ming Dynasties:

From 1279 to 1368 A.D., the Mongol tribe established the *Yuan* Dynasty. They were the dominant people of China during this time. There were only subtle changes in civilian costume. Men continued to wear their letter case, money packet, mirror bag, etc., on their waist and government officials wore identification badges of carved ivory or black wood. Women wore the seven necessities, (made of gold, jade, crystal, and rhinoceros horn in different shapes, carved into mountains or cloud patterns) with small hanging gadgets. The original meaning of these waist hangings was maintained; the seven necessities also came to be called the "golden seven" or the "golden four". Brocade bags stuffed with incense, (incense bags or dew-carrying bags), or bags filled with jewels and curios were worn on a woman's waist for decorative purposes.

Nine Official Wearings in the Ch'ing Dynasty:

With the advent of the *Ch'ing* Dynasty (1644–1911 A.D.) China had the last monarch. These rulers originated from the *Nu-Chen* (女眞) Tribe, a tribe from northeastern China who brought their leaders and their customs into central China. Still, much of the *Han* influence remained with the people.

Ch'ing Dynasty law specifically defined all aspects of costume with special regard to color in distinguishing rank. In the ninth year of the rule of Emperor *Shun-Chih* (順治) new laws were instituted defining the attire of government officials, merchants, and general civilians. The colors of an official's waist belt were chosen according to the standing of that individual. Bright yellow was the most noble color, golden yellow was second in importance with indigo blue as the third most important color. This belt was a silk fabric band connected with metal or gold decorative settings inlaid with jade. Purses were hung from metal rings extended from these settings.

In the early *Ch'ing* period, men had a choice of only two or three waist hangings. A greater variety of hangings developed in the later part of the *Ch'ing* Dynasty. These hangings were placed on both sides of his waist, the front collar at the right chest area. Women rarely wore purses; they wore mainly incense bags, and manicure tools extended from a lapel button. Men wore heart shaped incense bags, fan cases, eyeglass cases, a partitioned sheath holding chopsticks and a cutlery knife, watch pockets, and money pockets. This assortment was called the "nine official wearings". Smokepots, tweezers, and other small objects were also hung from the waist. *(see figure 10)*

By this time, purses had become more popular for their practical usage. The need was so great that shops in the larger cities were established to manufacture only purses. *Peiking's* purse-making industry was so lucrative that one street was named "Purse Alley". Writings found from the nineteenth century describe the manufacture of the nine wearings on Purse Alley. An extensive assortment of embroidered brocade and inlaid gold purses were created with great care. The demand for these meticulously fabricated purses was so great that one shop on Purse Alley, the *Long-Fu* Temple, was rumored to have copied the exceptional designs from the Imperial Court for purchase by common citizens.

Fig. 10

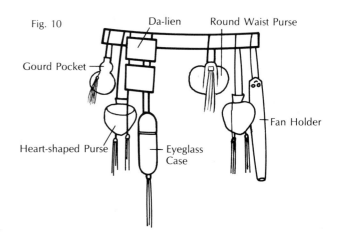

Da-lien   Round Waist Purse

Gourd Pocket

Heart-shaped Purse   Eyeglass Case

Fan Holder

In the book *"With the Dowager Empress"*, ①
Katherine Carl describe the Manchurians at the circus at the Summer Palace: "They wore the splendid summer court costume, embroidered in the double dragon,

Peddler Su Han-ch'en, Sung Dynasty

and for birthdays. The long hours spent on the intricate ornamentation shows how important and highly esteemed these accessories were. Many of these purses were made in the home by housewives and their young daughters.

It is customary in China that on the day of New Year's Eve the emperor would meet with his highly-ranked officials and servants and small embroidered purses were given to each one of them with a cache of small treasures, such as tiny charms made of gold or silver. These gifts were given as a symbol of good will and gratitude from the emperor himself. People who were fortunate enough to have this honor would wear it as a proud possession. These exceptionally beautiful bags were made by the masterful hands of court maidens and were meticulously embroidered with lush colors and auspicious motifs such as the *"Shou"* character, the phoenix, bat, the pairing of birds, the peony, etcetera.

① *With the Dowager Empress, Carl, Katherine
New York: The Century Co., 1905 (Page 224)*

reaching below the knee. They were tightly belted in around the waist, and very full and ample across the shoulders, giving the man the appearance, at least, of broad shoulders, and enhancing their already fine figures... The belt buckle, the handsomest ornament worn, was of carved jade, ruby quartz, or of beautifully chased gold set with precious stones. They were then wearing a profusion of ornaments dangling from their belts-embroidered cases for fans, chopsticks and knives, and many other ornaments besides the watch, an indispensable adjunct to every Chinese gentleman's costume. This is worn hanging from the belt in a handsome, embroidered case with an open front, so that the elaborate case, generally studded with jewels, beautifully enameled, or curiously incised, could be seen. This case had a sort of fob attachment made of silken cord, woven into quaint designs and finished generally with a wonderfully carved piece of jade, ruby quartz or some other curious stone."

These small purses served a wide range of uses. The special shapes acted as lucky amulets; holding flint and tinder sets, signature seals, watches, fans, eye-glasses. Traditionally, purses were given as special presents at specific celebrations. Such gifts were always very beautifully and heavily embroidered. They were also traditional gifts for children on the New Year

BIBLIOGRAPHY

Mailey, Jean, ed., **The Manchu Dragon.**
New York: Metropolitan Museum of Art, 1980

Chambers, M., Rawlings, C., Ritchie, M., eds.,
The Secret Splendors of the Chinese Court.
Denver: The Denver Art Museum, 1981

Chung, Young Y., **The Art of Oriental Embroidery.**
New York: Charles Scribner's & Sons, 1979

Shanghai: 1984 **Zhongguo Lidai Fushi.**

Goodrich, L., Cameron, N., **The Face of China.**
New York: Aperture, 1978

Carl, Katherine, **With the Dowager Empress.**
New York: The Century Co., 1905

Ken-Kai, Yang, **Tapestry and Embroidery in the Collection of the Museum of Liao-Ning Province.**
Tokyo: Grakken Tokyo, 1983

Chinese Periods and Dynasties

Neolthic Period..c. 5th millennium–18th cent.BC

Shia Dynasty...................2205–1766 BC

Shang Dynasty ....1766–1121 BC

Chou Dynasty ....1121–225 BC

Ch'in Dynasty...................225–207 BC

Han Dynasty....................207–220 AD

Northern and Southern Dynasties...220–589 AD

Sui Dynasty.....................589–618 AD

T'ang Dynasty ....618–906 AD

Five Dynasties..................906–960 AD

Sung Dynasty ....960-1279 AD

Yuan Dynasty................1279–1368 AD

Ming Dynasty ....1368–1644 AD

Ch'ing Dynasty..............1644–1911 AD

Chinese Symbolism

Most purses were given as gifts. These purses were decorated with symbols of good wishes and blessings as a warm gesture from the gift-giver to the receiver. Certain symbols were so commonly used that these decorations became a universal Chinese language used as decoration on china, furniture, clothing, and paintings.

The most frequently used symbols are listed below. Note that the Chinese used both Chinese characters and realistic objects as symbols for abstract words. Some objects were chosen because of the nature of the object while others were used simply because the pronunciations are the same.

Wan (萬) (Swastika): An ancient symbol for ten thousand.

Shou (壽): A Chinese character meaning longevity.

Hsi (喜): A Chinese character meaning happiness.

Shuang Hsi (双喜): A Chinese character meaning double happiness.

Fu (福): A Chinese character meaning good fortune.

Pan-Chang (盤長): The endless knot that is the Buddhist symbol for purity.

Fu (福): Good fortune, wealth
Pictorial symbols for good fortune, wealth:
Peony, phoenix, magnolia, begonia, Buddha's hand, gold fish, bat, old coins (money), gold nugget.

Lu (祿): Success
Pictorial symbols for success:
Dragon, deer, rooster, crest flower, crab, cricket, carp, pheasant, peacock, red apricot blossom.

Shou (壽): Longevity, health.
Pictorial symbols for longevity, health:
Chrysanthemum, peach, evergreen, bamboo, cat, butterfly, crane, tortoise, monkey, fungus, rock, sun, pine tree, swastika.

Hsi (喜): Happiness
Pictorial symbol for happiness:
Magpie, ching (musical instrument made of stone).

Ping-an (平安): Peace
Pictorial symbols for peace:
Vase, quail.

Ju-i (如意): Granting wishes

Ching (清): Pureness
Pictorial symbols for pureness:
Plum blossom, lotus blossom, orchid, narcissus, endless knot.

Chun (春): Spring
Pictorial symbols for spring:

Camellia, peach blossom, willow tree.

Duo-tzu (多子): Many children
Pictorial symbols for children:
Melon, pomegranate, day-lily, gourd vine.

Marriage: Pictorial symbols for marriage:
Mandarin duck, water lily

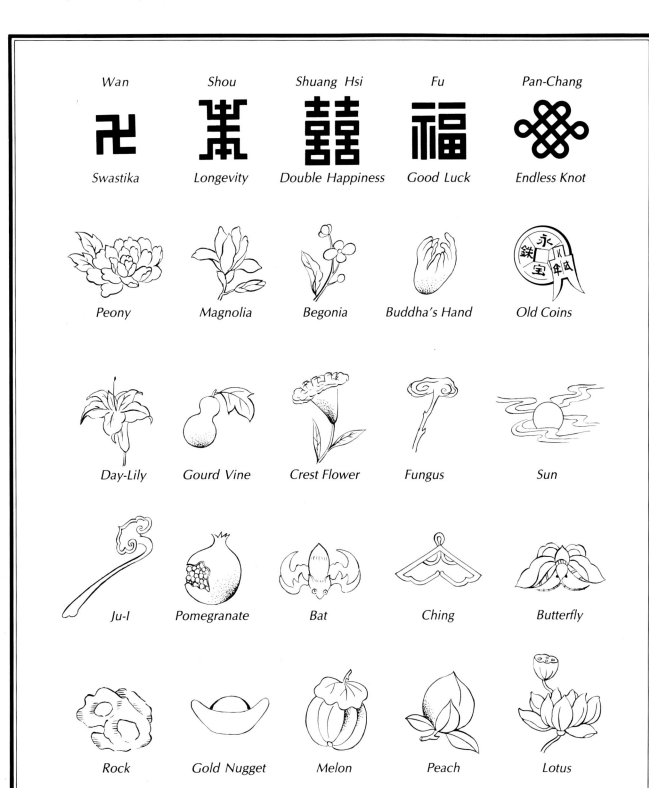

Wan	Shou	Shuang Hsi	Fu	Pan-Chang
Swastika	Longevity	Double Happiness	Good Luck	Endless Knot
Peony	Magnolia	Begonia	Buddha's Hand	Old Coins
Day-Lily	Gourd Vine	Crest Flower	Fungus	Sun
Ju-I	Pomegranate	Bat	Ching	Butterfly
Rock	Gold Nugget	Melon	Peach	Lotus

Chinese Embroidery

Excavations in the caves of Peiking *Chou-Ko-Dien* (北京周口店) uncovered bone needles used by the cavemen to sew animal skins over five hundred thousand years ago. Linen was created six thousand years ago in the *Yang-Shao* (仰韶) period, (painted pottery cultures, 4,000 B.C.). Over thirteen hundred years later, Chinese developed the silk fabric, made from the silkworm cocoon. In recent years, a small piece of silk was found; proving the origin of the craft.

The book, *Shang-Shu* (尚書), written two thousand years ago, provides the earliest known description of the embroidery made in the *Yu-Shuynn* (虞舜) period. Fragments of embroidered fabrics attached to bronzes dated three thousand years ago show that embroidered techniques were in use as long ago as the era of the *Shang* (商) Dynasty.

The oldest detailed fragment of embroidered fabric was found in the *Tzu Tomb* (楚墓), dating back to the middle stage of the Warring States period of the *Chou* (周)Dynasty (500 B.C. to 225 B.C.). This fragment is an example of the advancement of the craft. Both this fabric and the fabric found dating back to the *Shang* Dynasty show that the chain stitch was used in the earliest stages of embroidery. Embroidered fabric was not very popular. Interest in the art was limited to the aristocracy during the period of the *Chou* Dynasty. A law of that time prohibited the sale of beads, jade, brocade and embroidered fabric to the general public.

The production of silk became an important occupation among the peasants only in the years following the Warring States period.

The early chain stitch, or the inter-locked stitch, underwent little change over the years and remained dominant into the *Han* (漢) Dynasty. New stitching techniques were developed in the Northern and Southern Dynasties to illustrate the popular Buddha and motifs of the human figure. New visual effects were achieved through the use of the satin stitch, the seed stitch, etc. After thousands of years of constant use, the chain stitch was gradually replaced with new stitching techniques. *Tang* (唐) Dynasty embroidery is usually a full picture created by shorter stitches, covering the entire surface of the fabric. Applique of gold and silver and beadwork was also commonly used.

In the *Sung* (宋)Dynasty, Chinese art reached a peak. The arts of calligraphy, painting, pottery, tapestry, and embroidery were perfected as never before or after in the history of art in China. The art of embroidery surpassed its decorative function when embroidered fine art paintings were commissioned by government officials.

Sung embroidery is characterized by exuberant pictures stitched in elegant, delicate colors. Needles were as fine as a strand of hair and only one or two strands of yarn were used per stitch.

Yuan (元) Dynasty was ruled by the Mongolians and the arts of China had declined. The embroidery had become rougher than ever before.

In the *Ming* (明) Dynasty, the art of embroidery was revived. The most famous were the ladies of the *Ku* (顧) families. The *Ku's* style consisted mainly of satin stitches supplemented by the seed stitch and the stem stitch, with even more lustrous colors than those of *Sung* Dynasty art. Different textural effects were achieved by the use of a variety of materials. Artisans used silk, bird feathers, (e.g. the siamese fighting hen's tail, peacock feather...), gold leaf and human hair. Although less delicate than *Sung* embroidery, (at times these artists would even use a brush to paint in colors), the art of the *Ming* Dynasty was far richer in texture and color.

Embroidery styles of the *Ch'ing* (清) *Dynasty were* named after the areas they emerged from: *Su* (蘇), *Yueh* (粵), *Ching* (京), *Su* (蜀), *Shiang* (湘), *Wen* (溫), *Ming* (閩), styles. Methods and motifs of embroidery differed from place to place with new methods of stitchery always developing.

Chinese daughters were taught the art of embroidery at a very young age. Embroidery was considered a woman's craft and representative of her virtues. The works the young girl created over the years became a part of her dowry. The women from poorer families often brought in income from their craft, as a talented woman was well respected.

In a traditional Chinese house nearly every item made of fabric would be embellished with stitchery; cushions, tablecloths, curtains, door hangings, tapestries, screens, sheets, bed coverings and pillows. Clothes were embroidered. Formal costumes, caps, shoes, wallets and sachets all had to be embroidered in beautiful patterns. The great demand for decoration kept every woman busy with her embroidery frame for every moment of her spare time.

Tools and Materials Used in Embroidery

The tools:

The tools used to embroider are: a frame, (a wood stretcher used to secure the cloth and keep it taut), metal needles, a yarn cutter, pin cushions, and paper design patterns.

Frames are usually in rectangular shapes. Although the round frames are available, they are not frequently used. The rectangular frames are adjustable and do not damage the silk cloth as the round frames could.

The earliest known needles were made of bone and animal teeth. In later periods, needles were made of brass and iron.

Transferring the design:

Women would usually use patterns made by others while the more expert embroiderers would draw their designs directly onto the fabric. Several methods of tracing patterns onto fabric were used. The traditional method of transferring a design onto the cloth was with a cut stencil. The artist cut the design out of heavy weight paper with a sharp blade. The stencil was laid down on the fabric and oyster shell powder was dusted over the stencil. The stencil was removed and a powdery outline remained on the fabric. The artist painted over the powdery lines with oyster shell paste and brushed away the remaining powder. Another method was to loosely stitch through the thin rice paper outlines onto the fabric and remove the paper, leaving the stitched outline. Motif shapes could be applied to fabric with paste. The artist would simply stitch over the shape. This was the simplest and easiest method with no drawn lines left to mark the image.

The materials:

Silk yarn and fabric were supplemented with other materials to achieve special effects. Twisted silk yarn and untwisted silk yarn were both used. The untwisted yarn could be separated into finer strands to create a smooth, delicate surface. Twisted yarn was thicker and used to portray rougher textures such as bark and rock.

Silk satin fabric was favored. Gauze was often used for cross-stitching. Damask was also popular.

Some of the materials used in embroidered effects:

Additional materials were used to create special effects. Gold and silver were commonly used. Feathers, coral, pearl, human hair and a variety of other precious stones were used too.

Gold Chips: Gold leaf was pasted on paper or sheepskin.
Couched Gold Thread: Gold foil cut into small strips wrapped over silk yarn.
Gold Wire: Gold plated wire of brass or silver.
Peacock Thread: Twisted thread made out of peacock's feathers.
Hair: Infant's hair used as thread. Infant's hair was much softer.

Types of Stitches

It is not advisable to knot the end of the thread when beginning an embroidery stitch, this produces a coarse surface. Thread the needle, leaving an inch of thread on one end, with a few short stitches, tack the end of the thread onto the cloth and start to embroider. the end of the thread will be hidden in the embroidered surface.

The most commonly used stitches:

Stem Stitch (單線繡) or the Line Stitch: Used to embroider borders or fine lines.
Satin Stitch (平針繡): Stitches line up to fill the whole pattern; resulting in a smooth and shiny surface.
Long and Short Stitch (長短針繡): Generally used for large areas. This stitch created a 3-D effect and tonal variation.
Chain Stitch (鎖針繡): The needle is brought up and down, leaving a loop. The needle is brought up at the top of the loop, securing it with the next stitch. If the loops are interlocked, the stitch is called the "interlocked chain stitch".

Couching Stitch (灑線綉) or Laid Work Stitch: The rougher thread materials are secured to the fabric by this small stitch laid down in equal spacing.

Seed Stitch (打子綉) or Knot Stitch (結子綉): Bring the needle up through the fabric, firmly grasp the thread and loop it several times around the needle. Keeping the loop taut, re-enter the needle near the point it was brought up at. To be effective, this stitch should be kept even. This is also called the Blind Stitch or the Forbidden Stitch. Because it was so damaging to the eyes, young girls were often forbidden by their parents to practice this stitch.

Pekinese Stitch (北京綉): Originally practiced at Peiking, this is a back stitch that is placed down, and loops are threaded through the stitches.

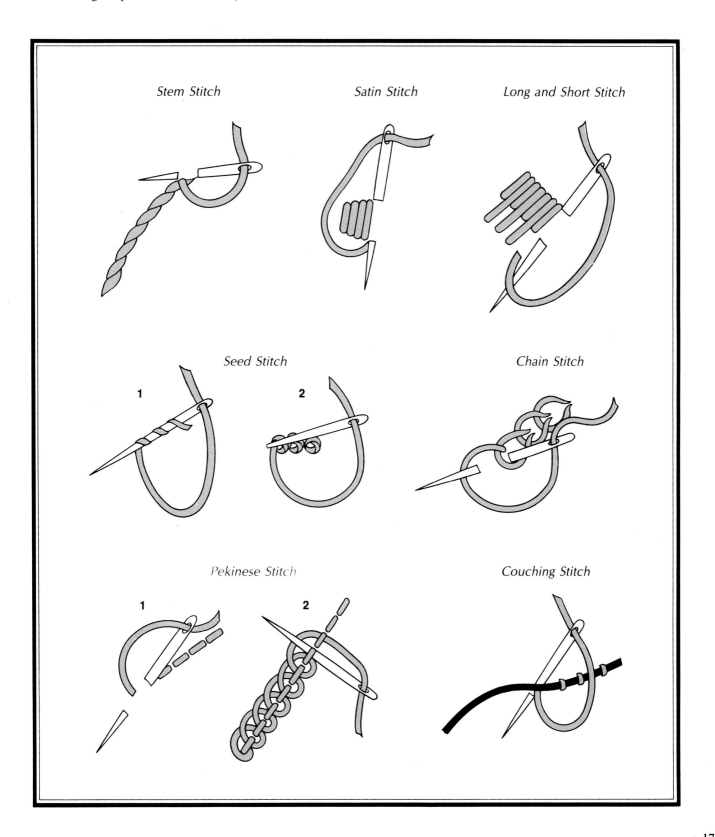

Stem Stitch

Satin Stitch

Long and Short Stitch

Seed Stitch

1

2

Chain Stitch

Pekinese Stitch

1

2

Couching Stitch

The Heart Shaped Purse

The heart shaped purse, also called the incense purse, was used as a sachet for both men and women. (This purse served the purpose that cologne does today). These purses were usually made in pairs, the colors of both purses identical with both sides often constructed in two contrasting colors. When hung off the waist, the colors of the purse(s) alternate as the wearer moves.

These purses were also made in the shape of kidneys and gold nuggets. The purses were lined with paper and made rigid at the pleated opening with rice paste. A piece of thread was tied around the pleats and sewn through the gathers with an intricately knotted cord attached.

The pouches were usually filled with cotton and incense. Beads were strung on the silken cord. These are the most decorative of all the Chinese purses.

PURSE WITH POEM ON BLACK SATIN
Poem is written in running hand and embroidered
with buttonhole stitches. Colorful tassles contrast
with the solemnity of the black and white purse.

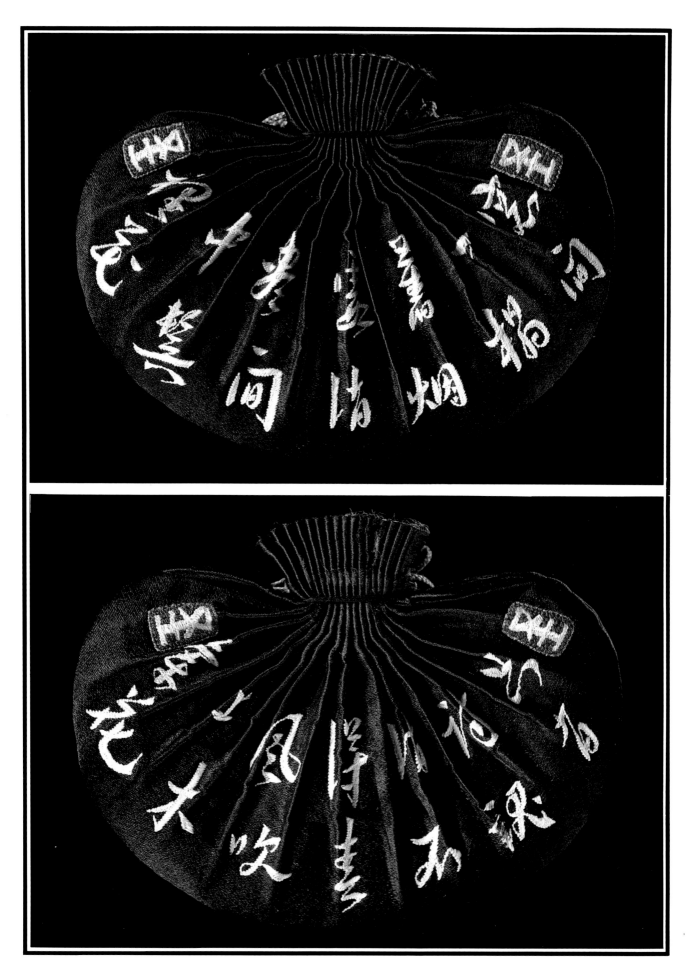

DETAIL OF CALLIGRAPHY

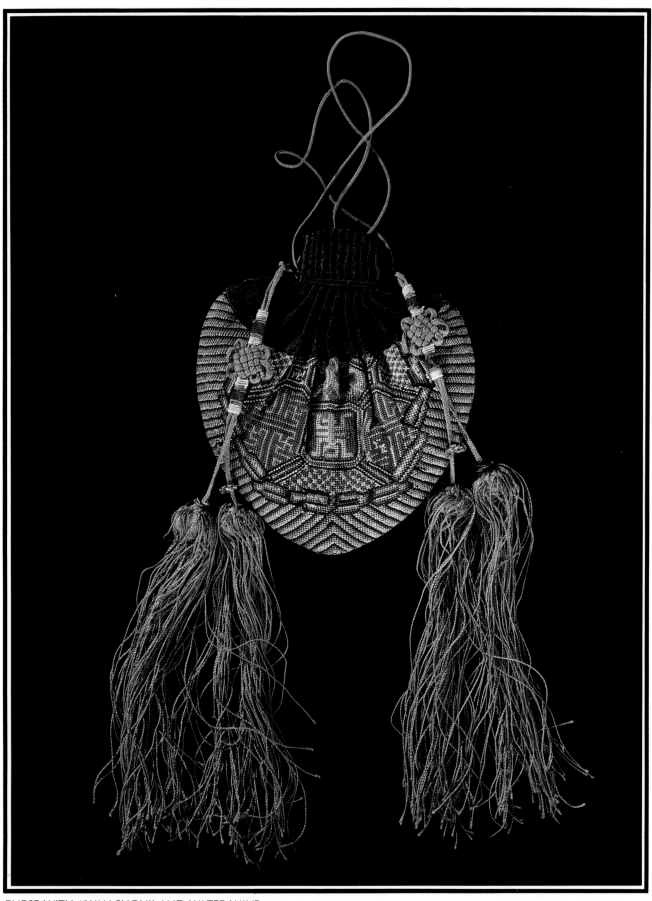

PURSE WITH "WAN-SHOU" AND WATER WAVE
Petit-point embroidery on gauze. The character
"Wan-Shou" means longevity.
(actual size)

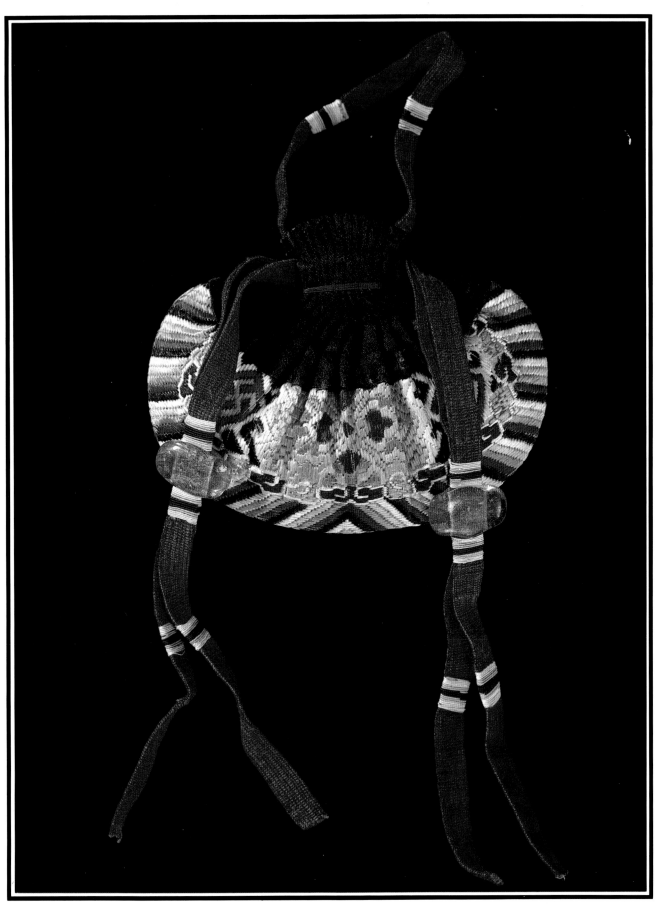

PURSE WITH PEONY AND SWASTIKA
Petit-point embroidery on gauze. The beads were
made of glass.
(actual size)

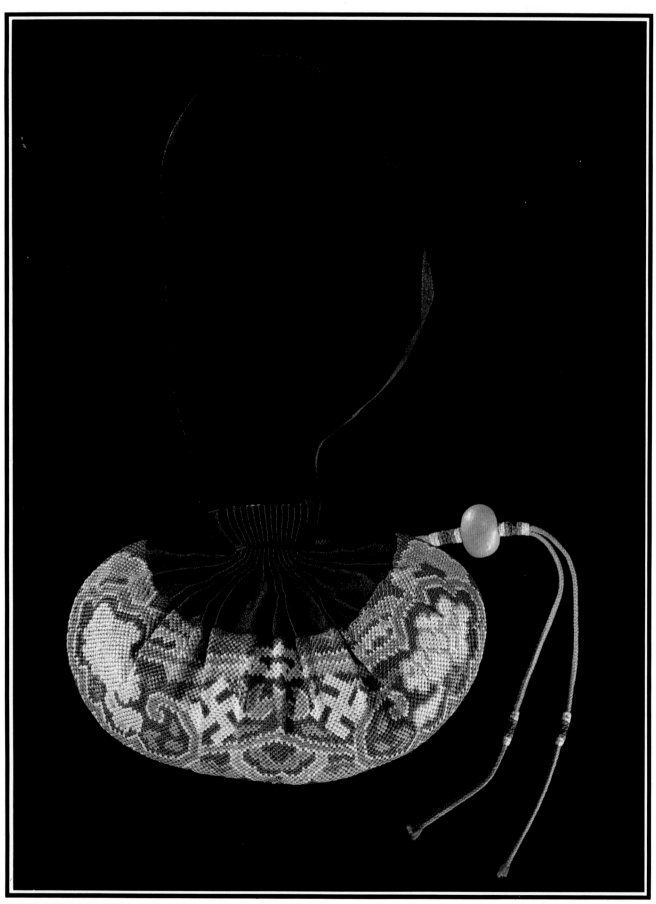

PURSE WITH SWASTIKA AND BAT
Petit-point embroidery on gauze. "Swastika" was
introduced to China around 200 B.C. Bats are
symbol of good fortune. (actual size)

PURSE WITH "WAN-SHOU" AND WATER WAVE
Petit-point embroidery on gauze. This stitch was
once popular during Chia-Ching（嘉慶）period
(1796-1820 A.D.) of Ch'ing Dynasty. (actual size)

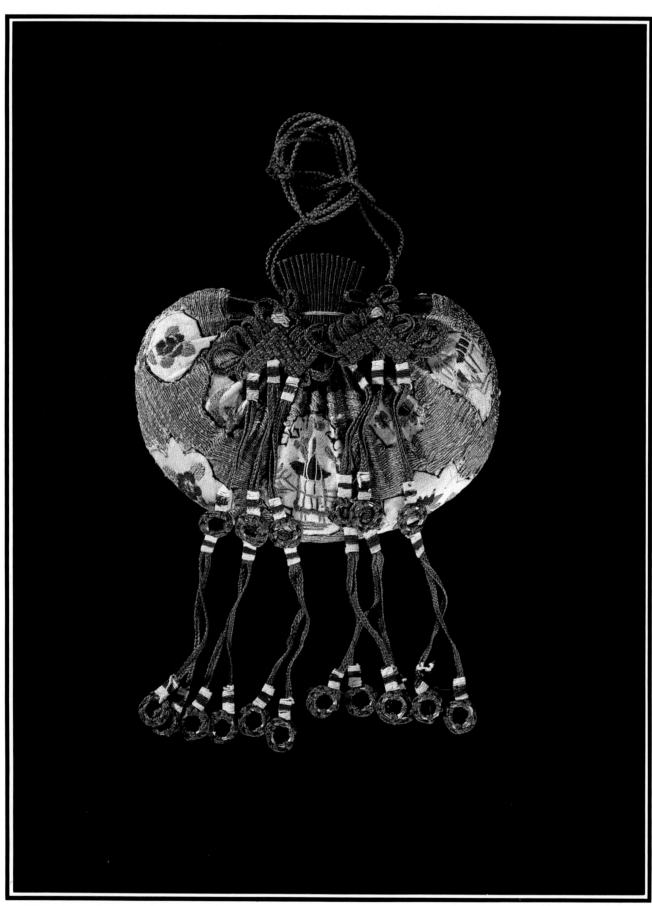

PURSE WITH SCENIC ON GOLD
Gold foil wrapped thread was couch-stitched on
the field. (actual size)

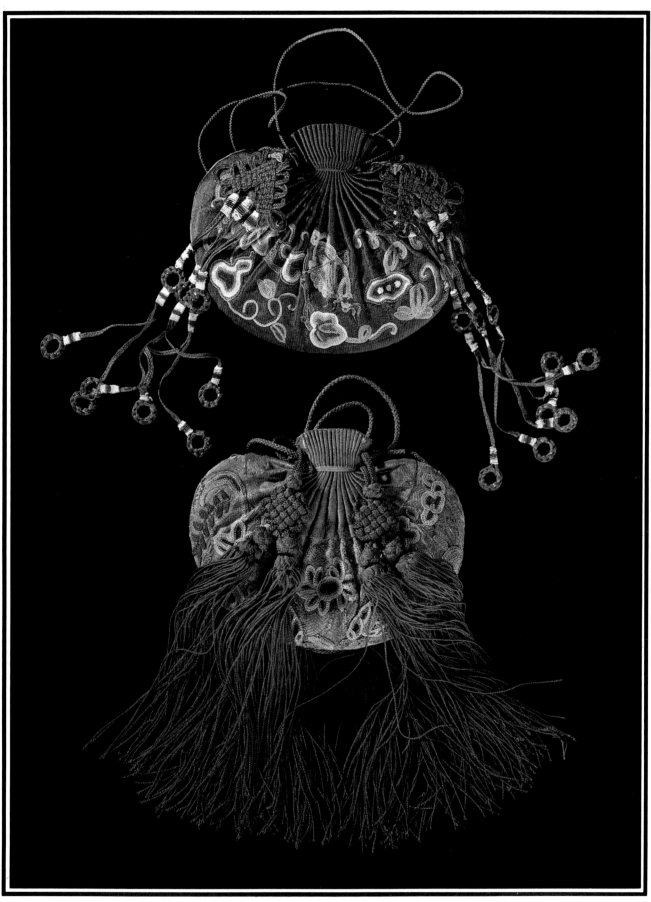

PURSES WITH GRASS AND CRICKET
Pekinese stitch and couched gold thread.

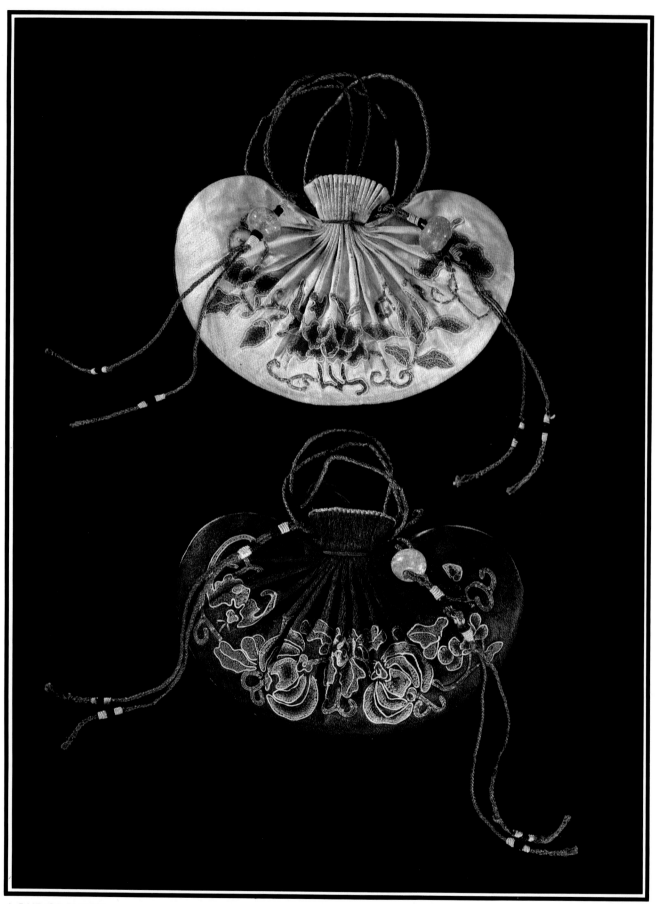

A PAIR OF PURSES
The pair is identical and each has different colors
on both sides. The melon and vine motif represent
the growth of family.

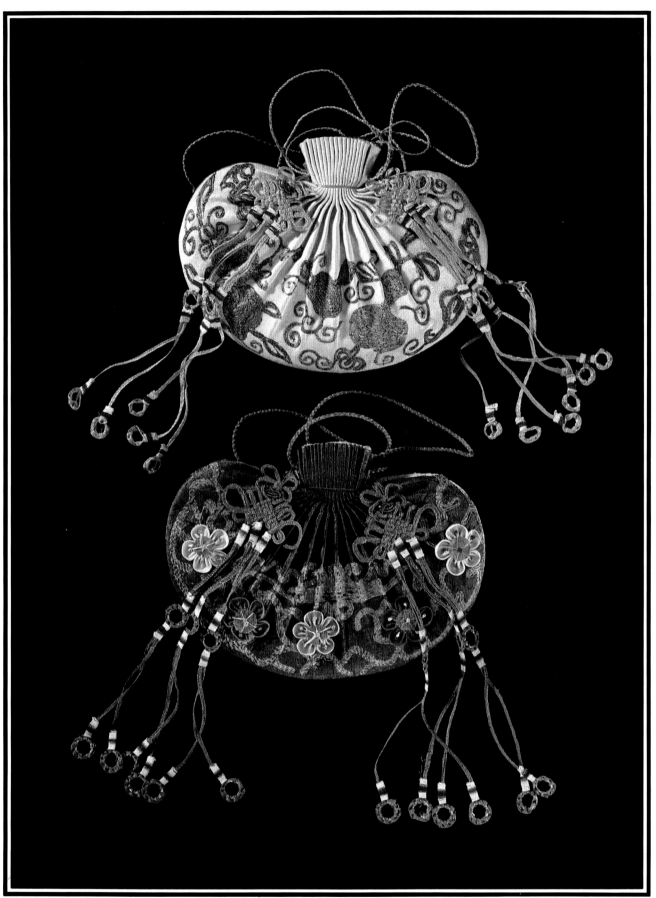

PURSE WITH MELON
Couched gold and silver thread. The many seeds
of the melon represent the hope of having many
children.

PURSE WITH PLUM BLOSSOMS
The flowers were individually made with silk fabric
and then attached to the purse.

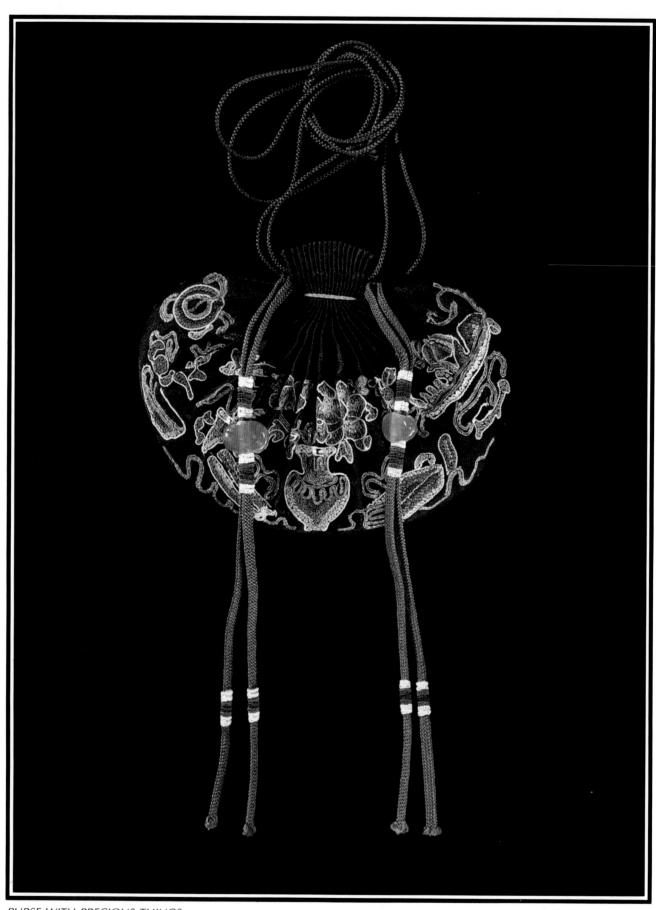

PURSE WITH PRECIOUS THINGS
Seed stitched with couched gold outline. The motifs
are an assortment of objects symbolizing good
fortune. (actual size)

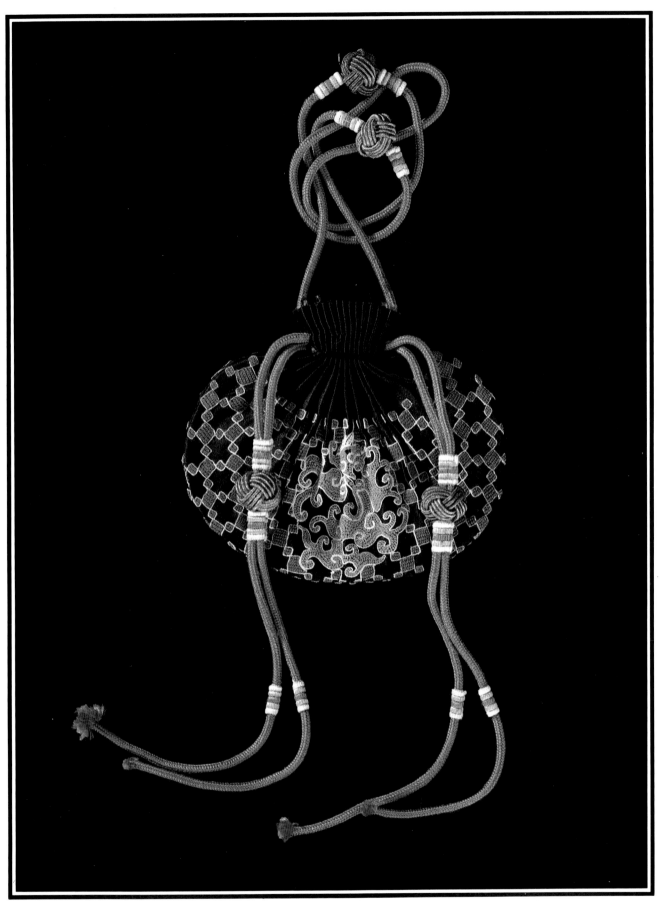

PURSE WITH DRAGON
The center of the purse is a delicately seed stitched
dragon.

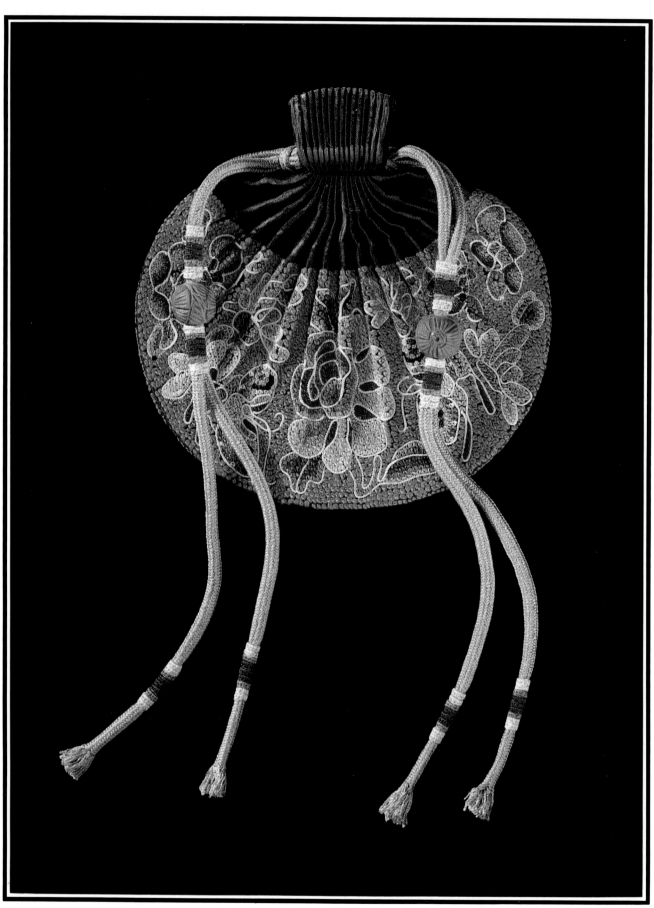

PURSE WITH PEONIES
The butterfly and peony are the most popular motifs
for embroidery. The purse is completely covered
with seed stitch (actual size)

PURSE WITH PEONIES
This seed stitched purse has two unusual knotted
tassles incorporated the Chinese character for "happi-
ness".   (actual size)

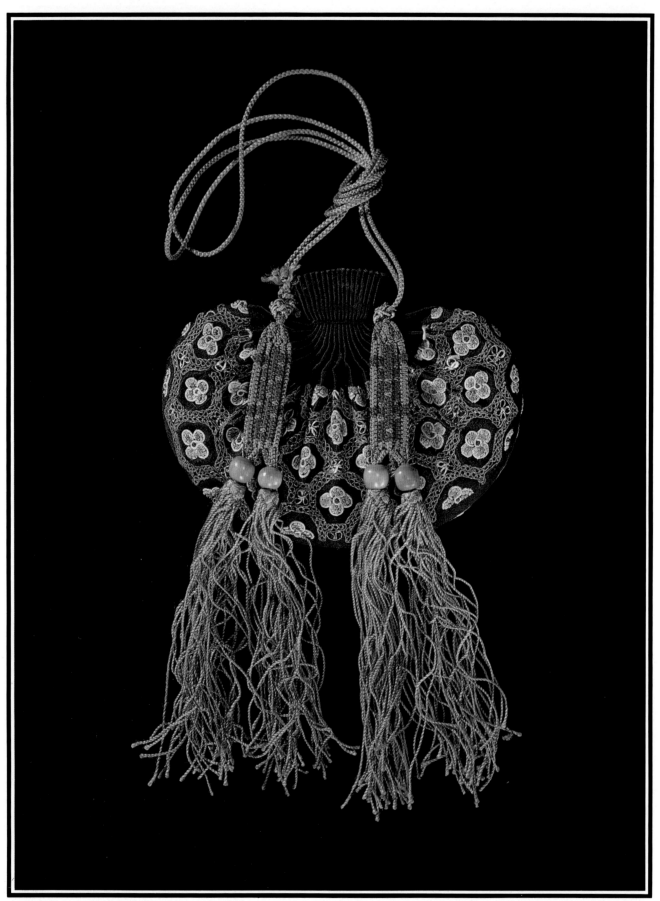

PURSE WITH ALLOVER FLORET
Embroidered with Pekinese stitch and seed stitch.
The two braids are knotted to form the character
''Happinese''. (actual size)

34

PURSE WITH ALLOVER FLORET
Embroidered with Pekinese stitch. The wood beads
are dyed to simulate coral. (actual size)

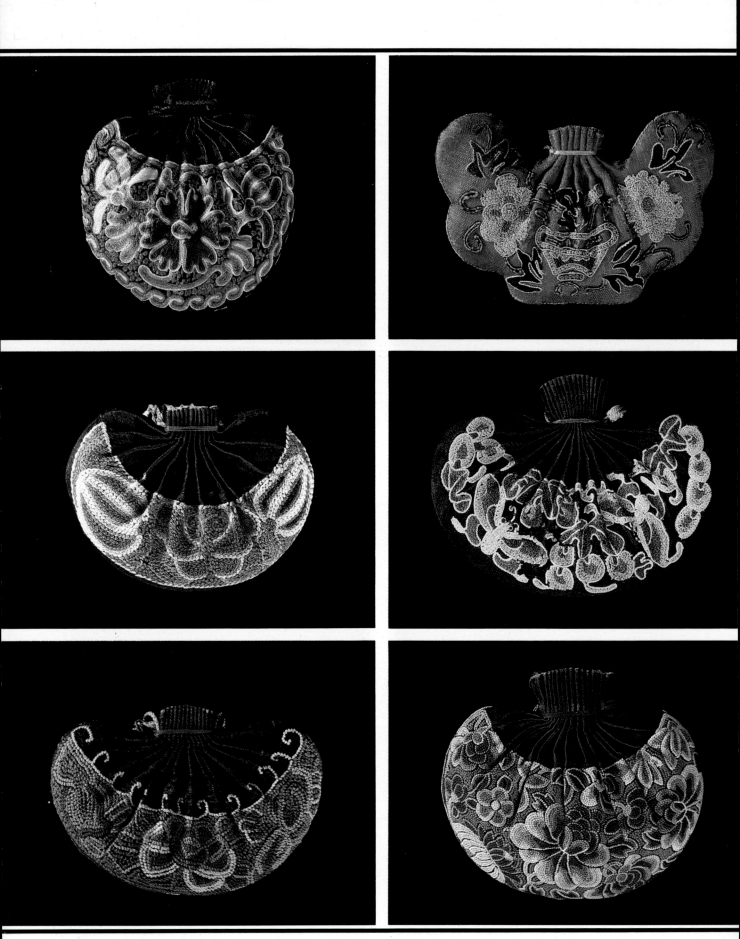

PURSES OF VARIOUS SHAPES
These purses are heart-shaped, kidney-shaped,
round, and even gold-nugget shaped.

PURSES WITH CALLIGRAPHY
Poems and proverbs were often embroidered on
purses for the beauty of the calligraphy.

The Eyeglass Case

Eyeglasses were introduced to China during the *Ming* Dynasty. Not every person who needed a pair was able to afford them as the natural crystal of the lenses was very costly. The affluent owner of a pair of eyeglasses was regarded with great esteem. Consequently, eyeglass cases became a valuable and elaborate ornament for every gentleman.

Early glasses were simple. Tender wire connected crystal lenses. The glasses were very small when folded. In the later part of the *Ch'ing* Dynasty, the glasses had frames, much like today's models.

There are three kinds of eyeglass cases shown here. One type opens at the middle, a second type has a pull-out opening at the bottom, the third type of case opens at the top. The shapes may range from oblong to rectangle.

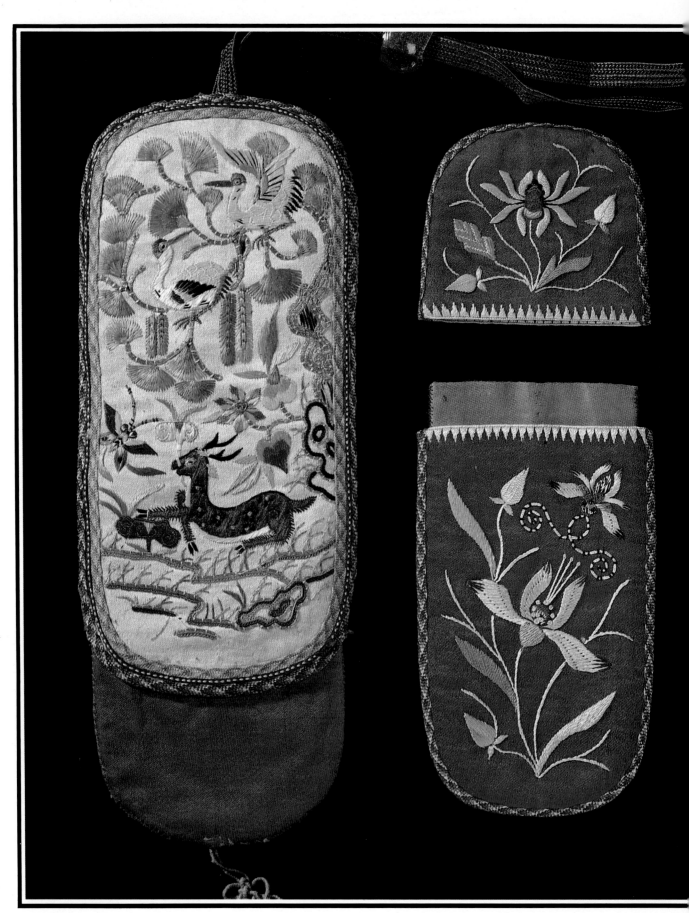

EYE-GLASS CASES
Deer and crane are symbols of good fortune, longevity
and health.
(actual size)

Round Waist Purse

These are often depicted in the old paintings, specifically paintings of the Nomadic costume. The purses were commonly seen on the *Dei-Hsieh* (蹀躞) belt.

There is only one decorated face on the purse and it has divided pockets in the interior. The oval frontpiece is reinforced with cardboard backing.

The top of the purse is slightly wider than the bottom.

This allows the top to be pleated and fastened by the hanging cord when actually worn. Most of the round waist purses shown in this book are new, never worn, so there are no visible pleats to shorten the shape of the top.

PURSE WITH A PAIR OF LION CUBS
The cubs were stuffed to become three dimensional.
Embroidered with seed stitch. The border has lace
work with silver foil showing through.
(actual size)

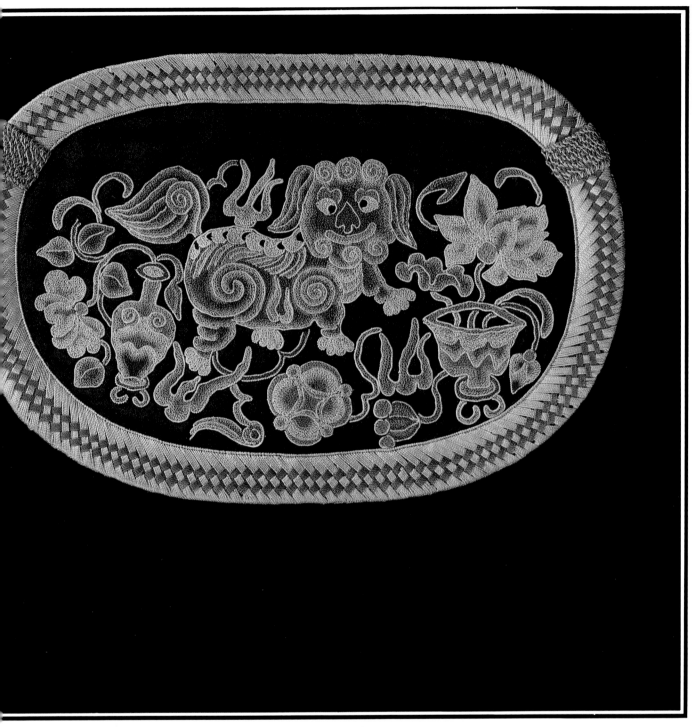

PURSE WITH FU LION
Embroidered with seed stitch. The lion romping
with brocade ball is a common theme of peaceful
joy.
(actual size)

(MAGNIFIED DETAIL)

45

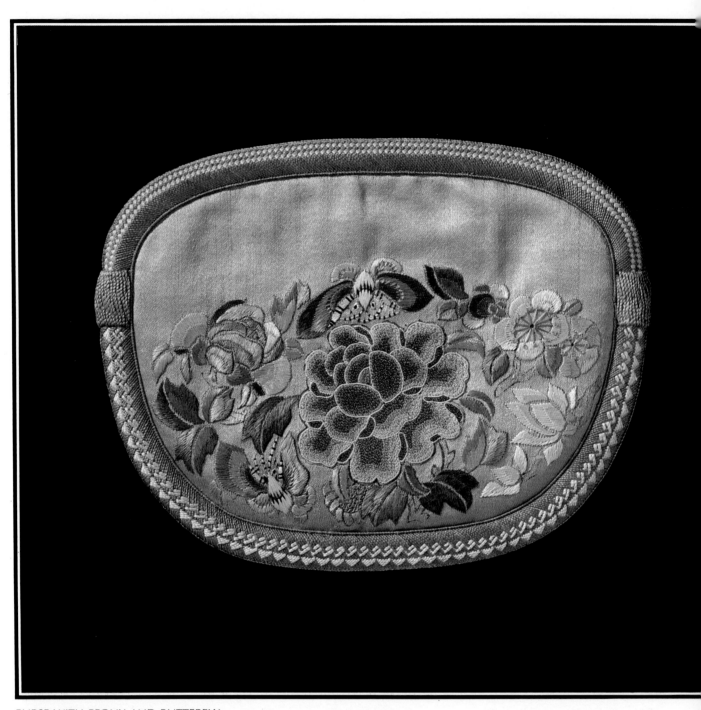

PURSE WITH PEONY AND BUTTERFLY
Peony is seed stitched. The background is done in
satin stitch.
(actual size)

PURSE WITH PEONY AND BUTTERFLY
Melon with its many seeds represents a happy family with many children. The butterfly and peony also give good wishes. The purse is completely covered with seed stitch.
(actual size)

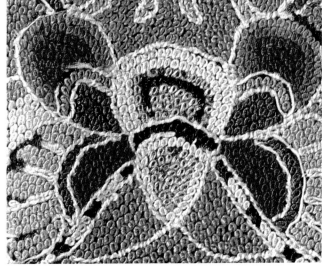

(MAGNIFIED DETAIL)

47

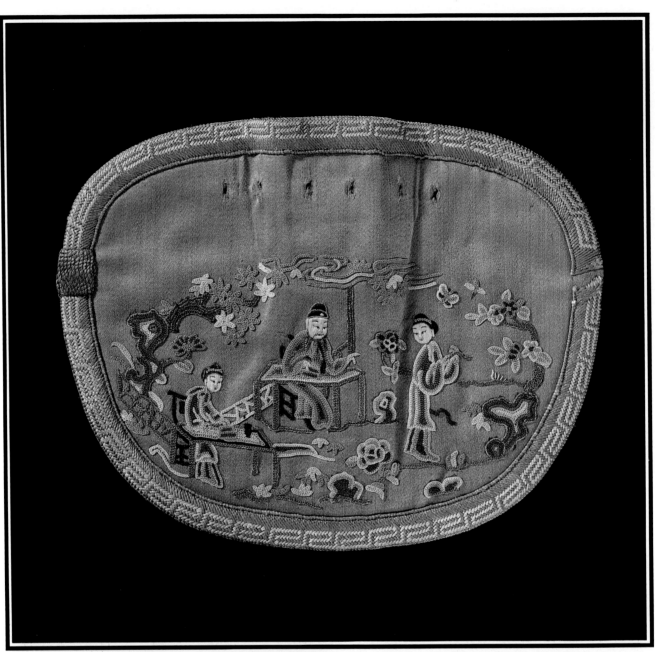

PURSE WITH THEATRICAL FIGURES
The scene is from a popular Chinese opera depicting a maiden accompanied by her servant, studying in the garden with her tutor. The whole purse was done in Pekinese stitch with the exception of the faces, which are in satin stitch.
(actual size)

(MAGNIFIED DETAIL)

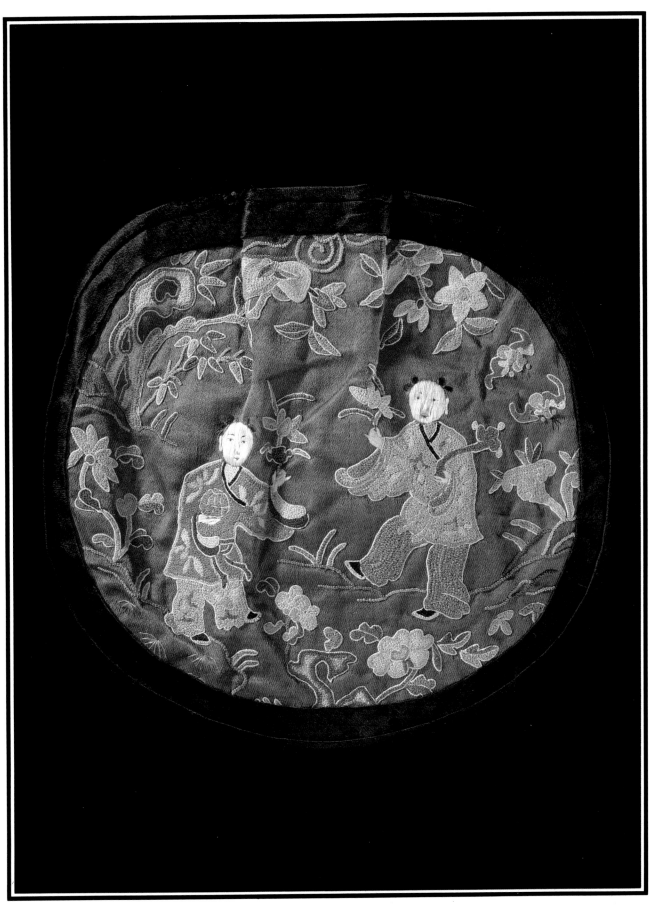

PURSE WITH MYTHICAL FIGURES
The two figures each holding a lotus blossom and
a round box were said to bring happiness to marriage.
This purse was done in seed stitch. (actual size)

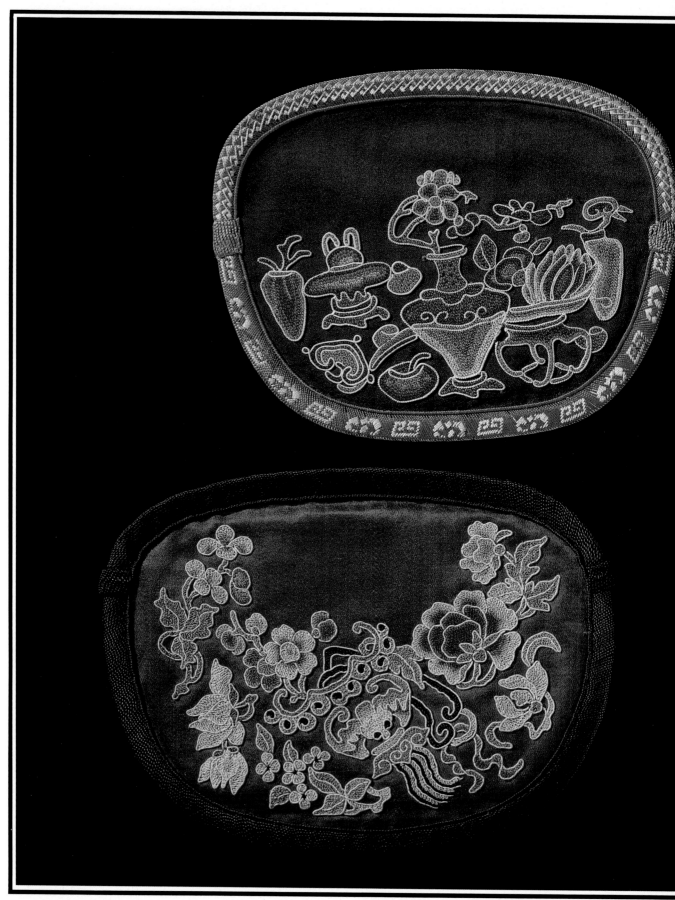

FOUR PURSES WITH PRECIOUS THINGS
There are an assortment of symbols of good fortune
on these purses: gold nuggets and coral trees for
wealth, peach and fungus for health, and bat and
buddha's hand for good fortune.
All four purses are done in Pekinese stitch.

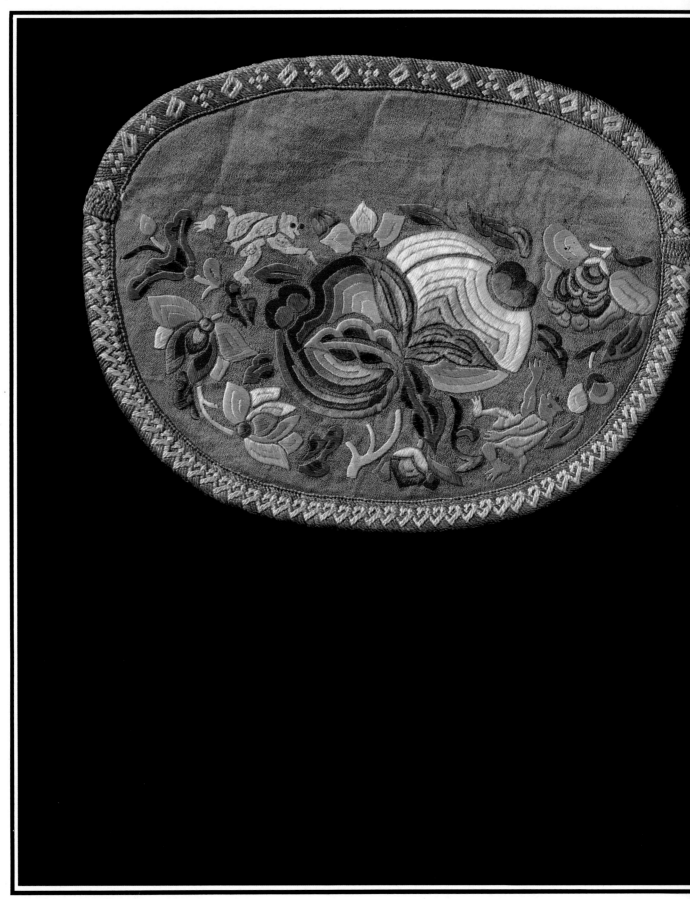

PURSES OF SATIN STITCH
The legendary monkey is said to have stolen peaches of immortality. The purse may have been a birthday present.

The phoenix is a mythical bird symbolizing peace and prosperity. (actual size)

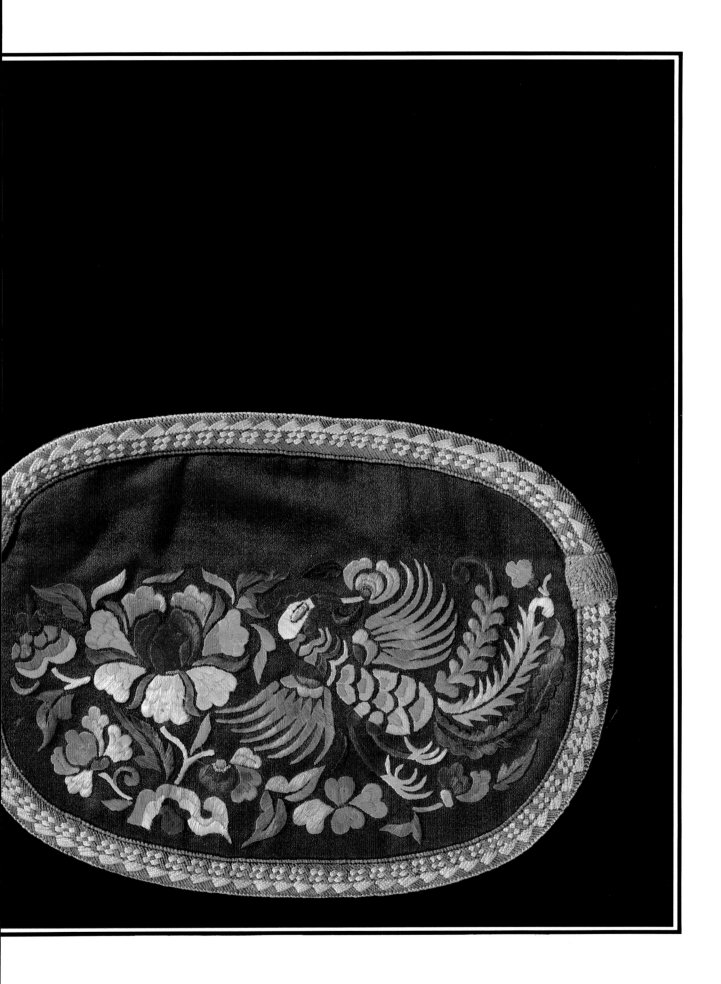

TWO PURSES OF UNUSUAL SHAPES
The left one has two button loops, probably used
to fasten to the skirt. The right one is shaped as a
butterfly. Both purses are in seed stitch. (actual size)

54

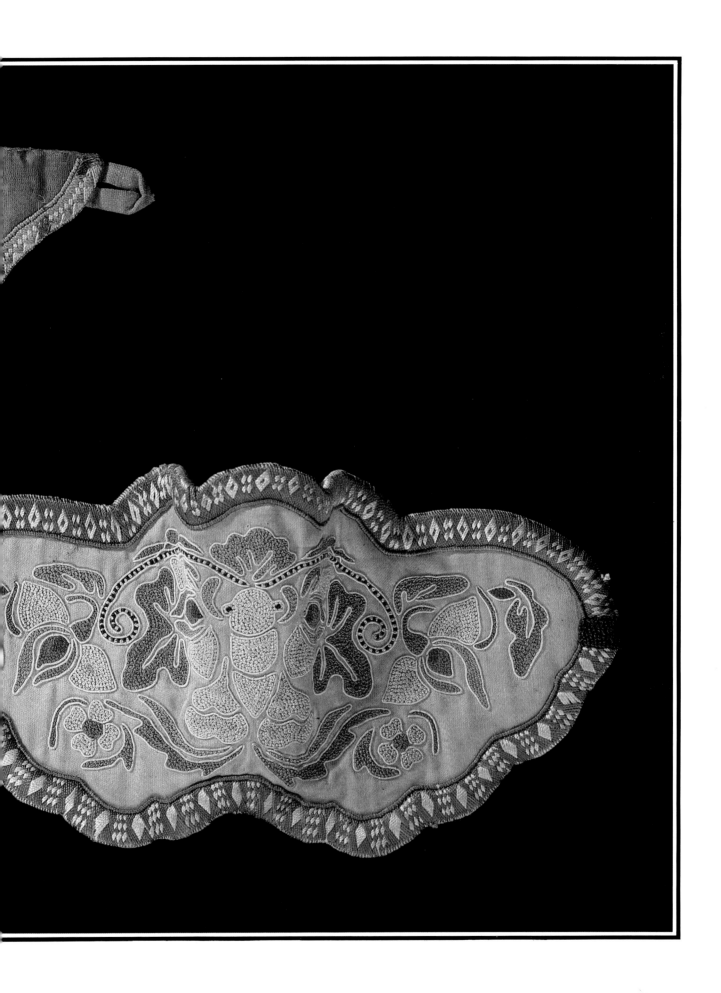

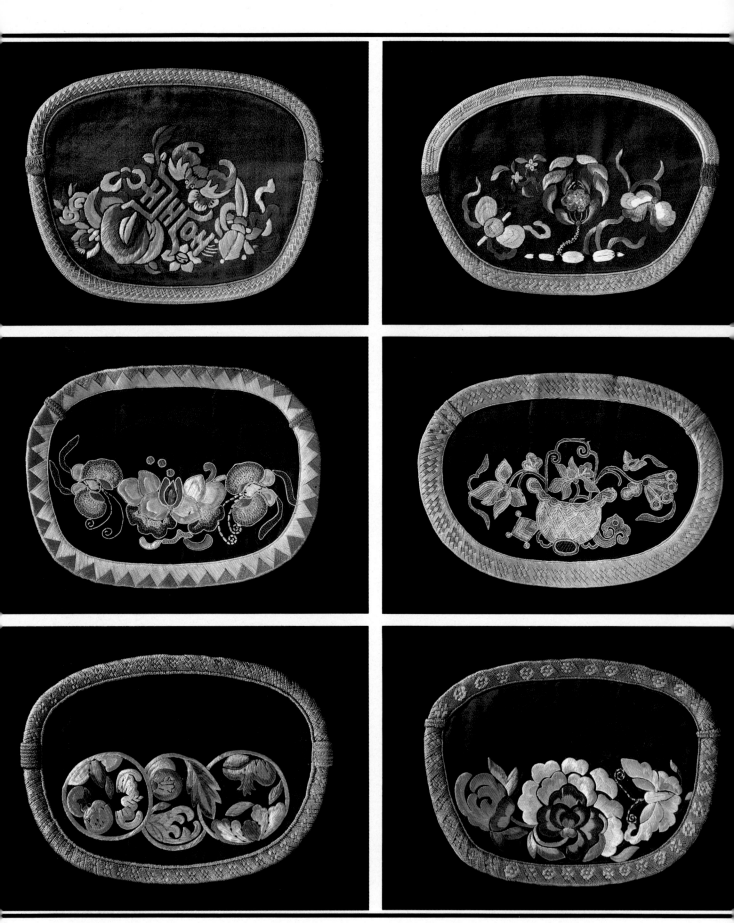

PURSES

Borders are often stitched with heavier thread of two colors interlocking to create a variety of interesting patterns.

Occasionally they are made in plain colors to contrast with a complex geometric pattern on the purse.

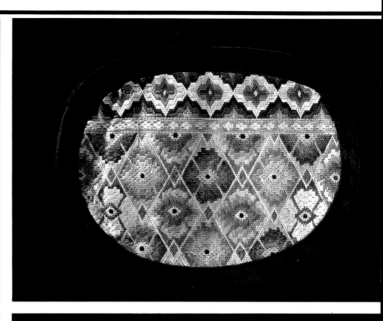

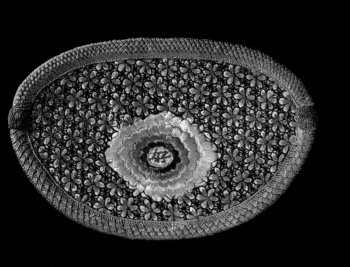

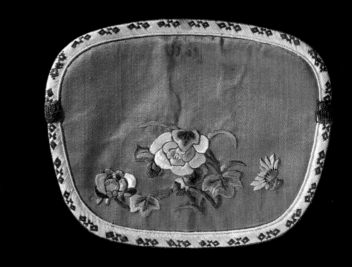

The Square Purse

If a purse was to substitute for a pocket, as in one theory, these purses would be the perfect example. These purses are embroidered on both sides and have a flap on the front and back. The purses split into three interior sections, and unlike the round shaped purse, both front and back are supported with stiff cardboard. A cord is passed through the top, over both sides, meeting at the bottom with a tassle.

There are also one-sided rectangular purses with a fabric top folding piece allowing the waist belt to pass through.

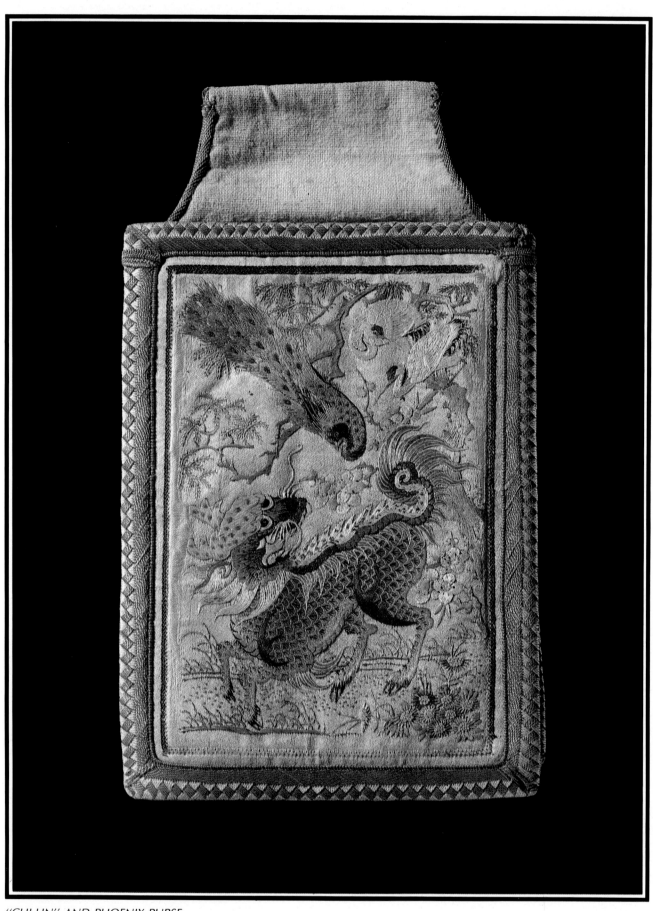

"CHI-LIN" AND PHOENIX PURSE
The mythical beast "Chi-Lin" is said to appear only
when peace is prevailing. (actual size)

This is a remarkable example of Ch'ing Dynasty embroidery, most certainly of imperial quality. (magnified detail)

PURSE WITH ROOSTERS AND ROCK
Rooster standing on the rock accompanied by cock's crest is a common theme of prosperity.
(actual size)

PURSE WITH THEATRICAL THEME
Embroidered with seed stitch. It depicts two men
and a woman in a journey. This purse has a primitive
charm in the rendering. (actual size)

PURSE WITH VASE AND PEONY
This still life of a vase holding peonies represents
peace and prosperity. Behind the vase is a stylized
"Ju-I". (actual size)

64

The purse is finely embroidered mostly in Pekinese
stitch and some seed stitch. It has a couched outline
of twisted white thread. *(magnified detail)*

PURSE WITH CRICKET AND GRASS
The crickets are first embroidered and then padded
underneath to give a raised look.
(actual size)

66

*Embroidered in Pekinese stitch and long and short
stitch. (magnified detail)*

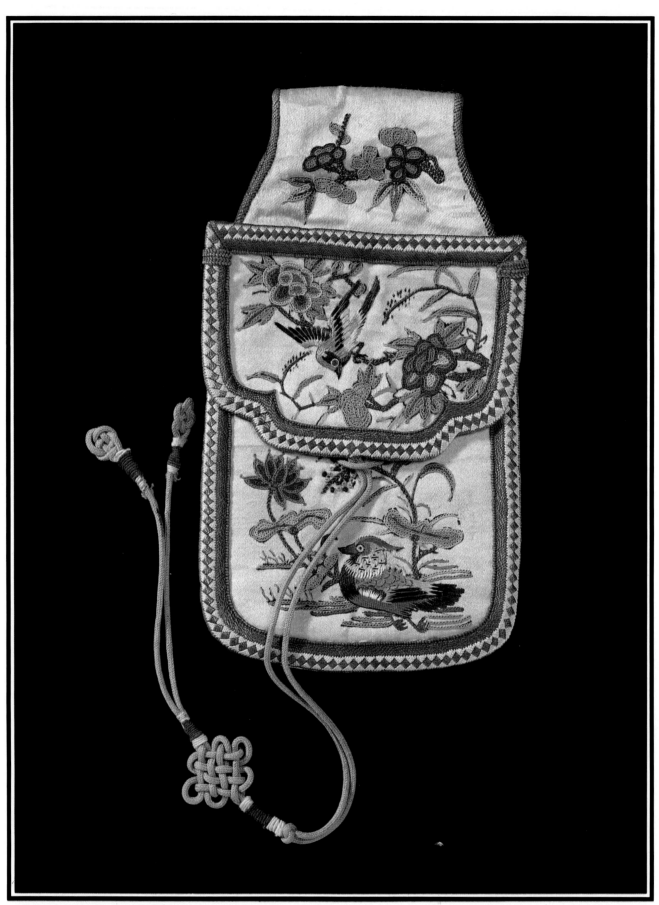

PURSE WITH BIRD AND FLOWER
Mandarin ducks and magpies are birds of happiness.
Purse is embroidered in Pekinese stitch and long
and short stitch. (actual size)

PURSE WITH BIRD AND FLOWER
Peacock is for prosperity. Embroidered with Pekinese
stitch and long and short stitch.
(actual size)

PURSE WITH MAGPIE AND ROOSTER
Embroidered with long and short stitch and Pekinese
stitch.
(actual size)

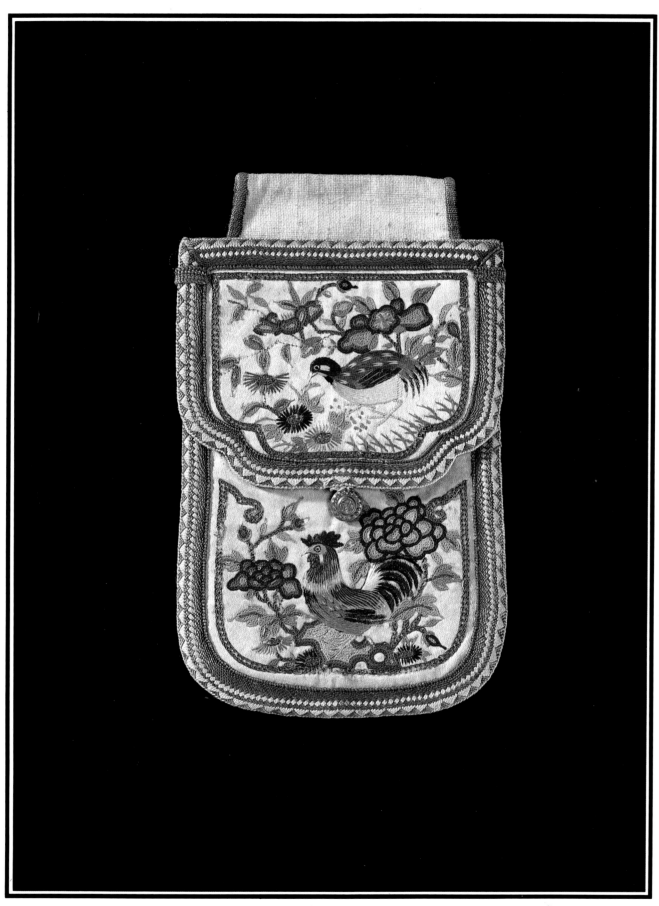

PURSE WITH QUAIL AND ROOSTER
Embroidered with long and short stitch and Pekinese
stitch.
(actual size)

PURSE WITH QUAIL AND KING-FISHER
Embroidered with long and short stitch and Pekinese stitch. The reverse side in black and white satin is embroidered with different birds. (actual size)

PURSE WITH ROOSTERS AND MAGPIE
Embroidered with long and short stitch and Pekinese stitch. The reverse side has different birds. (actual size)

PURSE WITH PHEASANT AND SONG BIRDS
*Embroidered with long and short stitch and satin
stitch. Reverse side shown on opposite page.
(actual size)*

PURSE WITH ROOSTERS AND PHEASANT
*Embroidered with long and short stitch and satin
stitch. Reverse side shown on opposite page.
(actual size)*

PURSE WITH ROOSTER AND MAGPIE
*Embroidered with long and short stitch and Pekinese
stitch.*
(actual size)

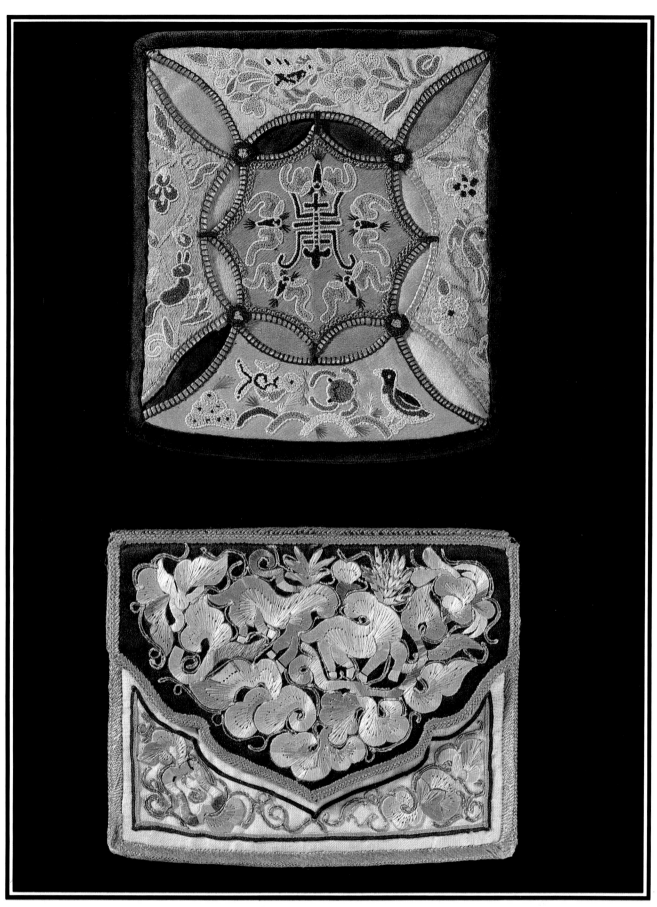

THE VARIATIONS OF SQUARE PURSE
The purse on the top is embroidered with seed stitch
in a patchwork pattern. Purse on the bottom is
embroidered with satin stitch. (actual size)

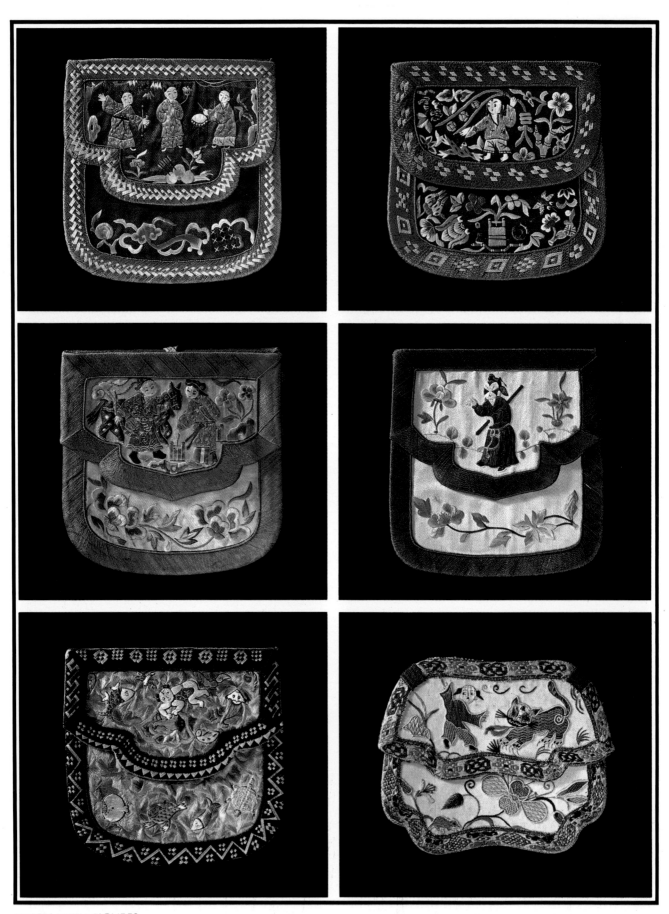

PURSES WITH FIGURES

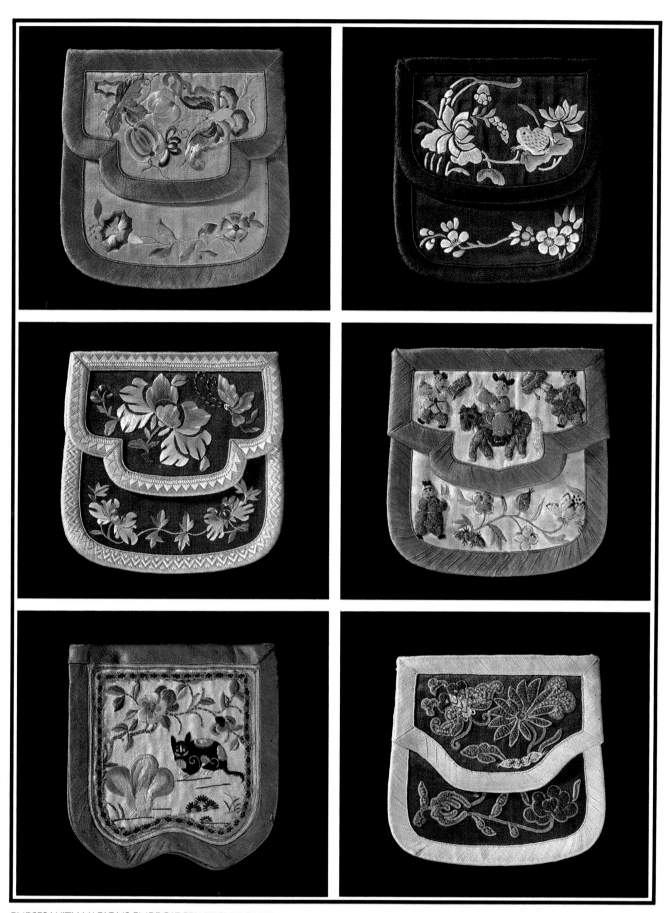

PURSES WITH VARIOUS EMBROIDERY TECHNIQUES

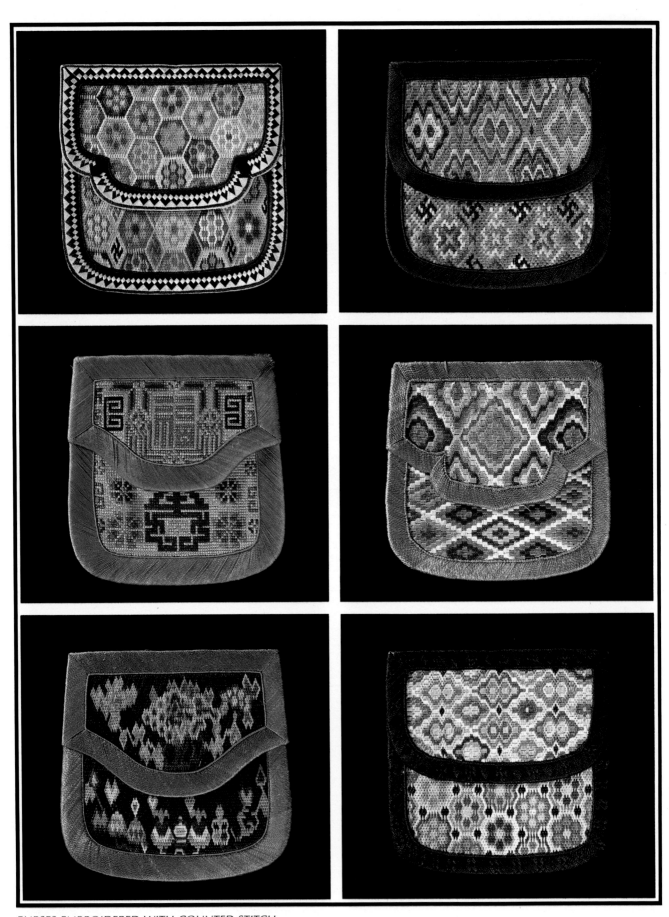

PURSES EMBROIDERED WITH COUNTED STITCH

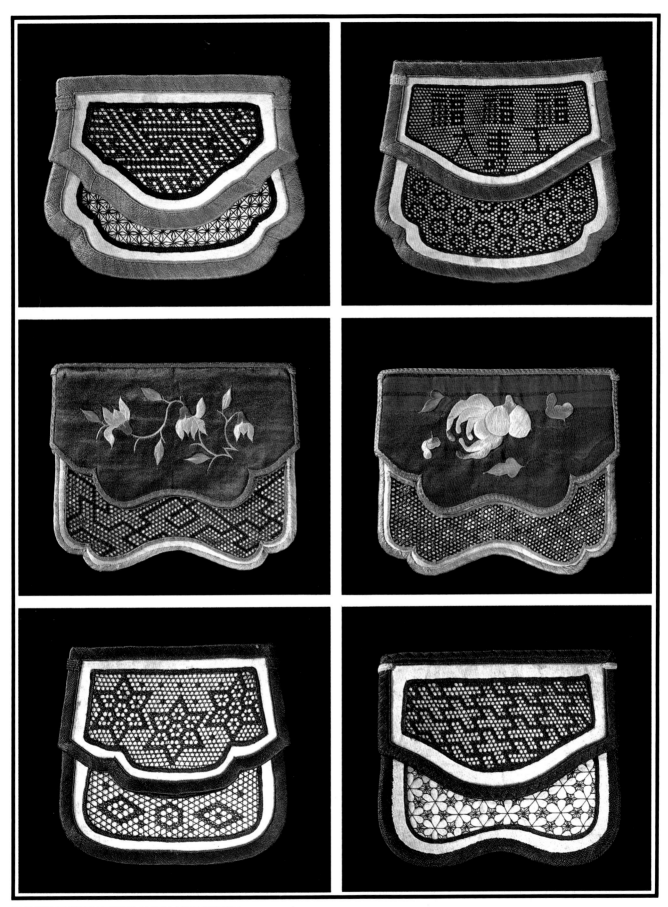

PURSES EMBROIDERED WITH NET STITCH

81

Da Lien

The *Da Lien* is an oblong soft envelope that flops over the waistbelt. The purse has a soft center envelope with a hard pocket on each side.

There is great variation in shape on the end pockets. These pockets are square, shaped like a vase, melon, etc. They are often strung with tassles.

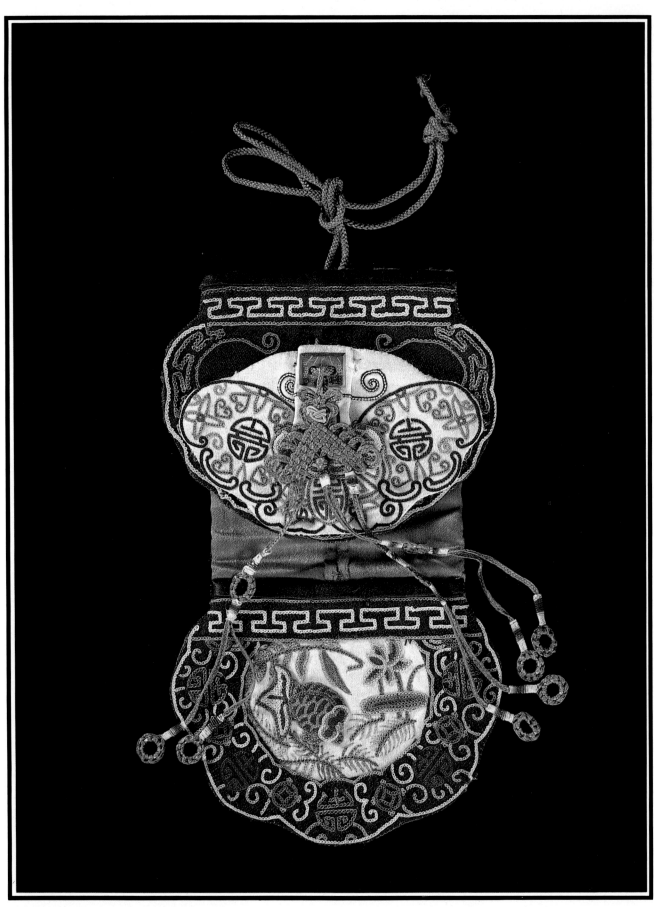

PURSE WITH GOLD-FISH AND BUTTERFLY
*Embroidered with Pekinese stitch and padded gold-
fish. (actual size)*

PURSE WITH CRICKET AND BEGONIA
Embroidered with Pekinese stitch. The top pouch
is shaped as a vase.
(actual size)

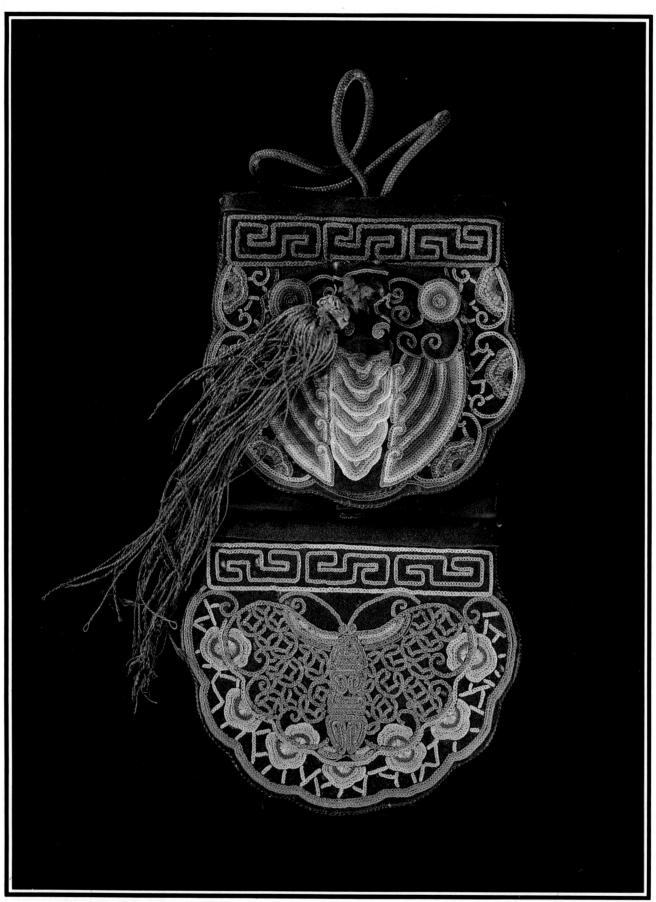

PURSE WITH BUTTERFLY
Embroidered with Pekinese stitch.
(actual size)

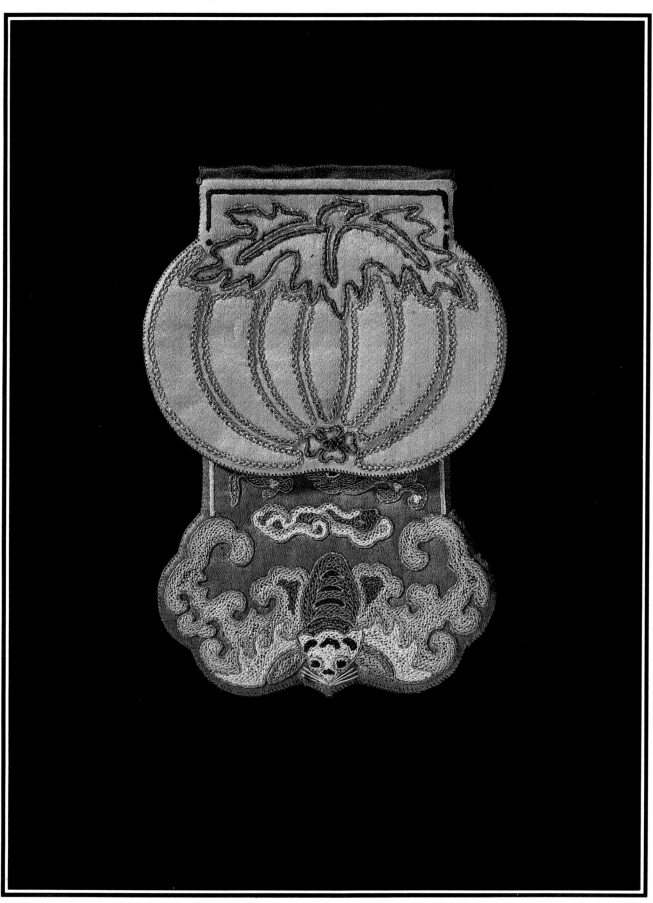

PURSE WITH MELON AND BAT
Embroidered with Pekinese stitch.
(actual size)

PURSES WITH CALLIGRAPHY
Embroidered with satin stitch.

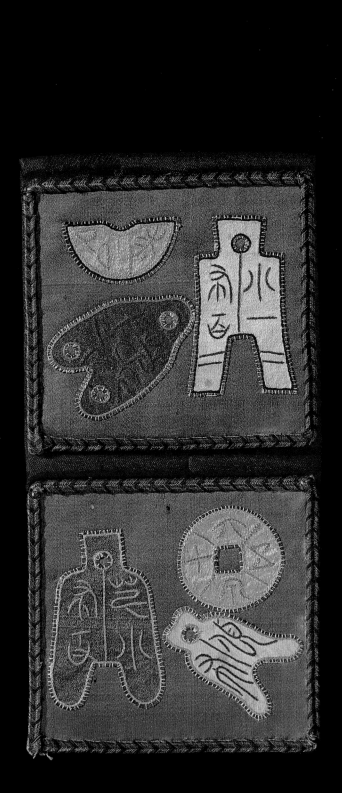

TWO PURSES
The purse on the left has appliques of ancient coins
outlined with chain stitch. The one on the right
is in chain stitch and couched gold.

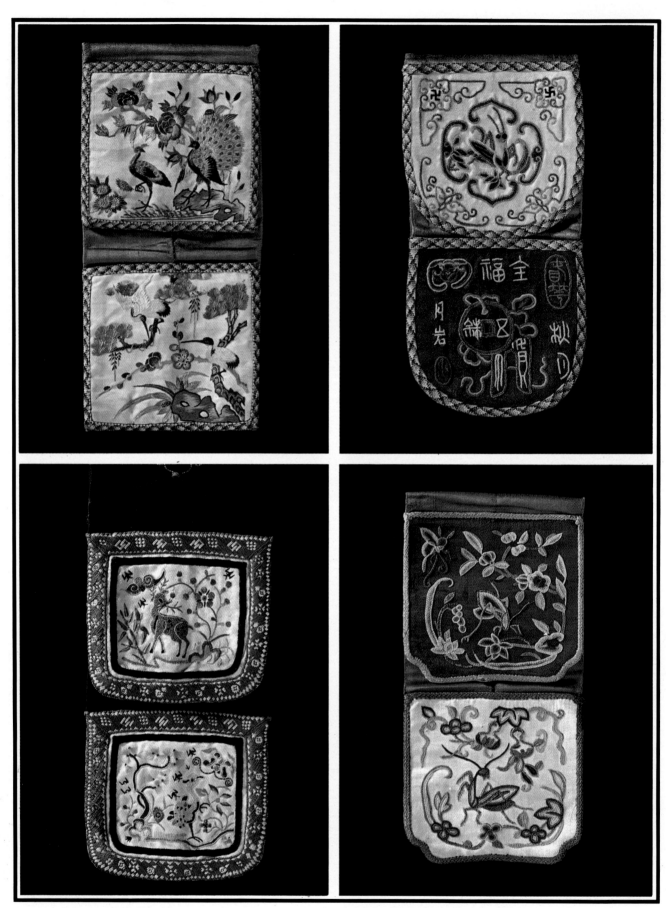

PURSES WITH DEER AND CRANE   PURSES WITH CRICKET AND GRASS

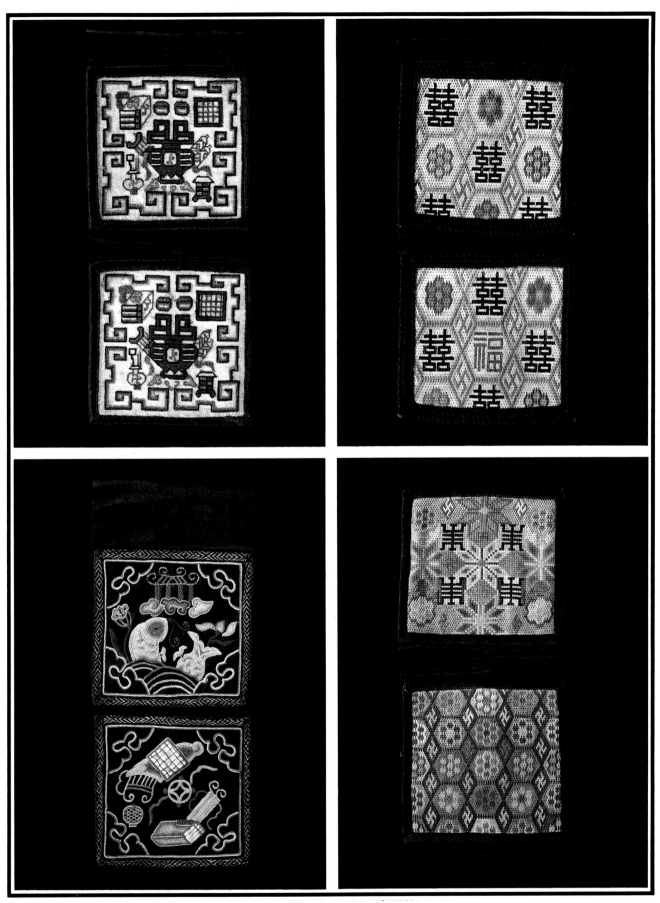

PURSES WITH SCHOLARS' TREASURES   PURSES EMBROIDERED WITH COUNTED STITCH

Gourd Pocket

The gourd pocket, used for holding tobacco, was also called the tobacco pouch. The gourd pocket was hung from the smoking pot. The pockets are in gourd shapes as the gourd was the symbol of medication in Chinese mythology. Tobacco was thought to be a healing drug. It became popular in the early part of the *Ch'ing* period and was commonly used by both men and women near the close of the *Ch'ing* period for recreational and medicinal purposes. Gourd pockets are long with an opening on one side near the top. The opening is just large enough for two fingers to fit through. These pockets were decorated on both sides, with four multicolored hanging tassles. The gourd pocket was also used for holding incense.

GOURD SHAPED PURSES
Left: Chain stitch with couched gold and silver
thread outline.

Center: Twisted thread with couched gold and silver
thread outline.
Right: Satin stitch with twisted thread. (actual size)

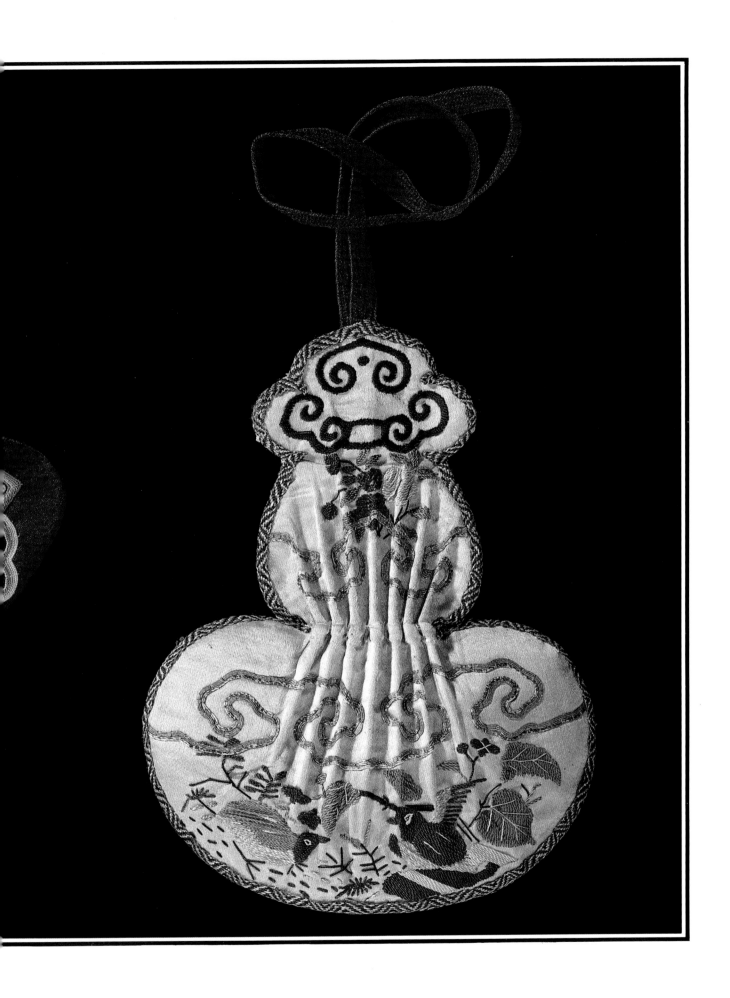

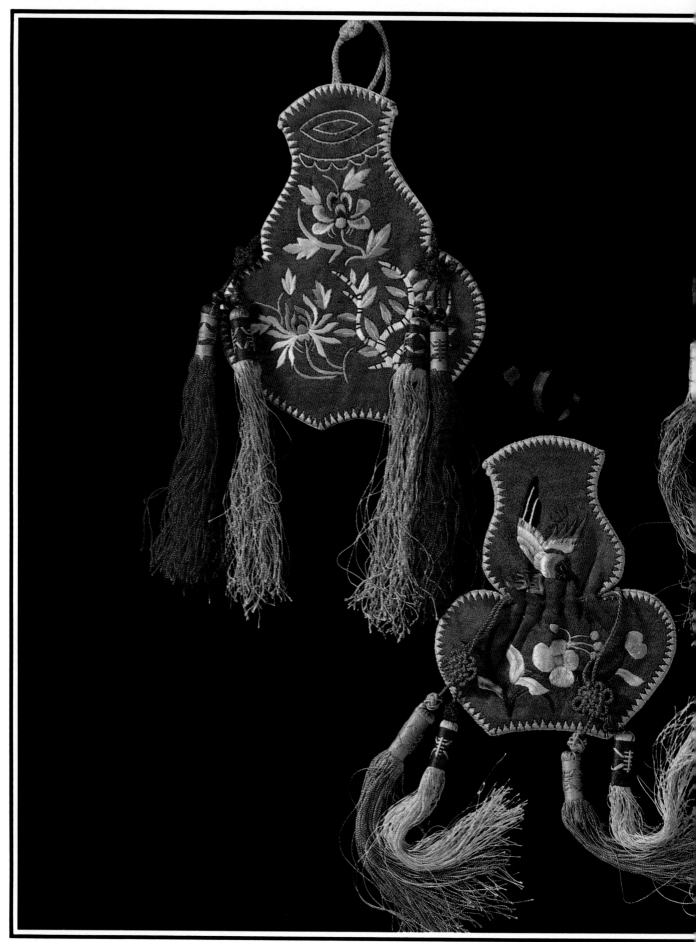

GOURD SHAPED PURSES

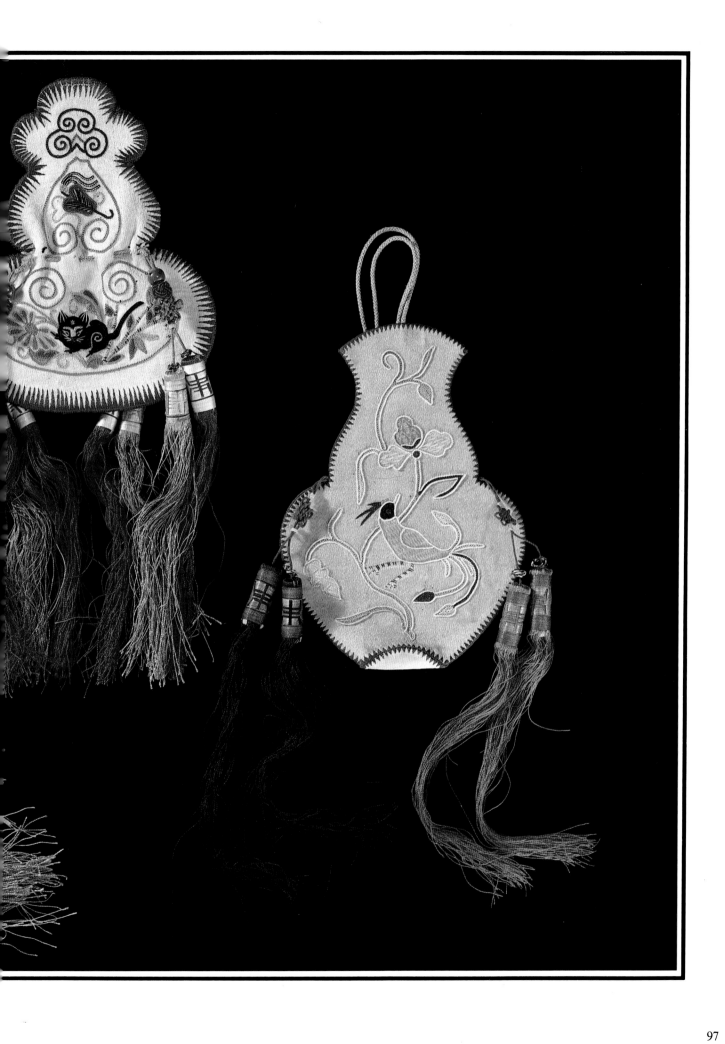

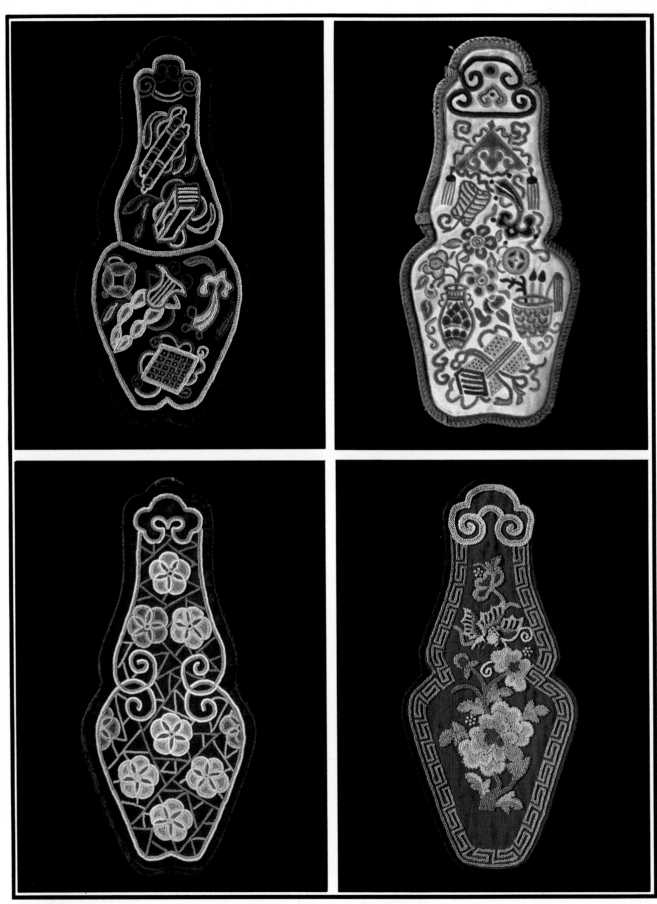

GOURD SHAPED PURSES
Embroidered with Pekinese stitch and seed stitch.

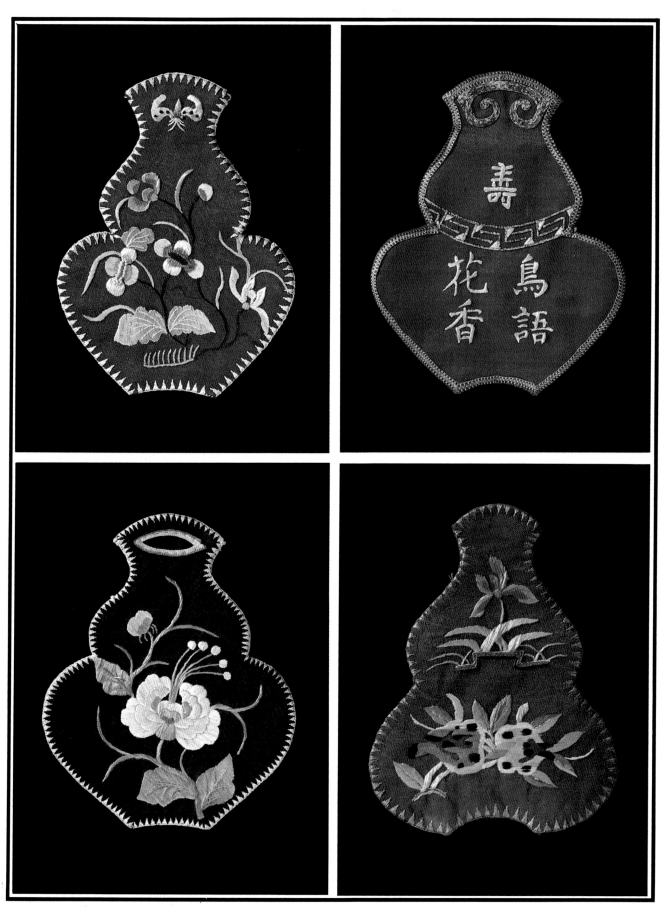

GOURD SHAPED PURSES
Embroidered with long and short stitch and satin
stitch.

BELL SHAPED KEY HOLDER
This type of purse has an opening at the bottom.

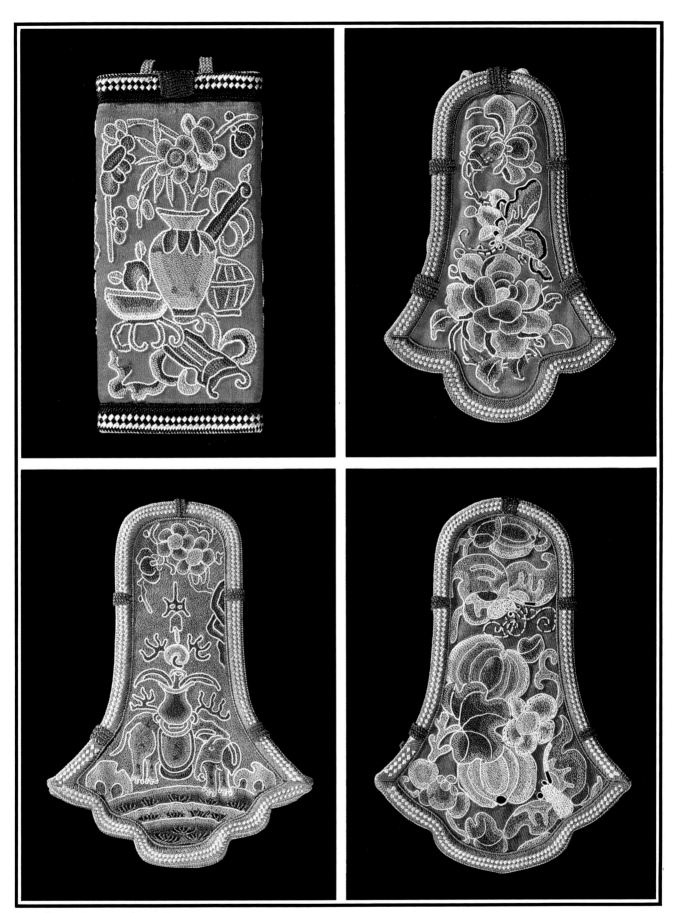

BELL SHAPED KEY HOLDERS
Completely embroidered with seed stitch. An
elephant carrying a vase is the symbol of peace.

Fan Holder

Fan cases are narrow and long with a small attached flat bottom, and cords for hanging. Fans were an important accessory for keeping the gentlemen cool in the summer. These cases are usually appliqued or embroidered with summer flowers for this reason.

Some historians have made the mistake of taking these cases for chopstick holders. Only the Manchus wore their knives and chopsticks in wooden cases to formal dinners, the majority of Han Chinese people did not.

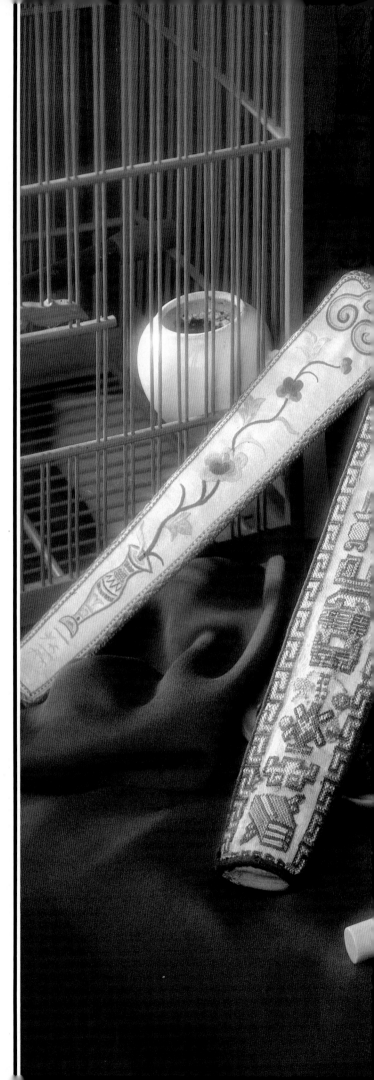

FAN HOLDERS
The black case has motifs favored by scholars; musical instruments, chess sets, books and painting scrolls.

The long fan holders at the center have applique of dyed fabric.

Letter Case

The letter case is a container for writings or documents. Constructed as cloth folders, they fold into two or three parts with hidden pockets, full pockets and half size pockets inside. The exterior is left undecorated but the interior is covered with elaborate and intricate needlework and colorful triming. The motifs were mainly of symbolism for men. The word "crown" (冠) (crest) of the rooster is homonymous with the word "leadership" (官). The rooster crest, and other types of crowns, therefore had the signifcance of success in the politcal sense.

Letter cases are as large as a book or as small as a wallet and only used by men.

THREE FOLD LETTER HOLDER
Auspicious motifs embroidered with satin stitch.
(actual size)

THREE FOLD LETTER HOLDER
Auspicious motifs embroidered with satin stitch.
(actual size)

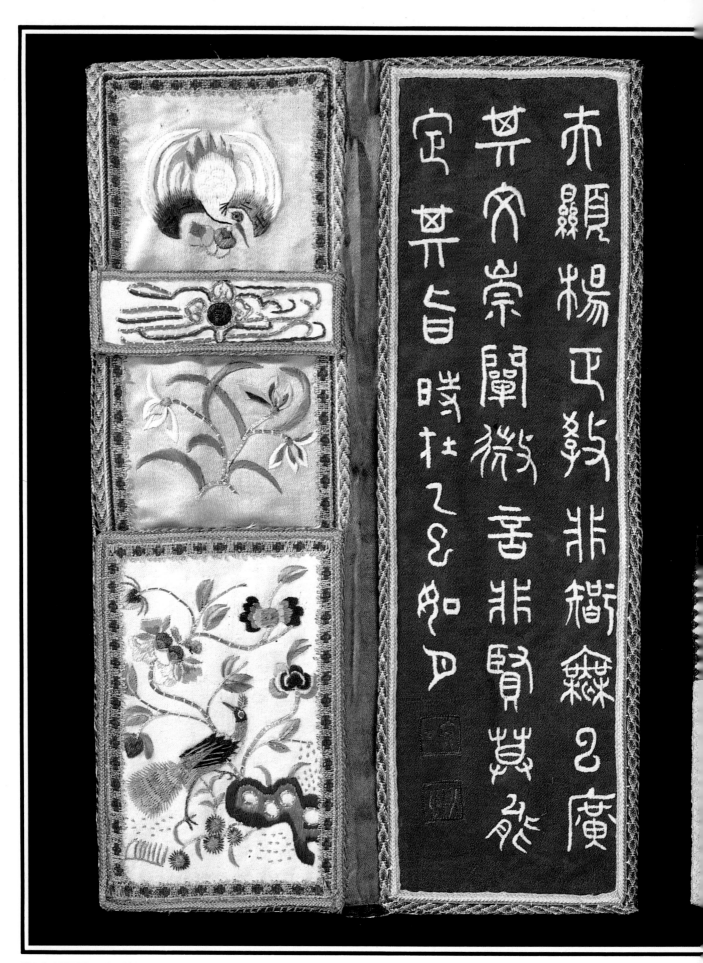

TWO LETTER HOLDERS

君子擇人
而後交
丁己孟春書

113

Instructions and Patterns

Although these purses are small, making each one was time-consuming. Not too many people in today's busy world can afford to spend days or weeks on one small object such as this. For the real enthusiast, however, the ancient method of purse-making is worth the time. Using some creativity, new materials can be used. Silk jacquard, print or woven fabric with small motifs are two ideas. A handmade gift of a purse always brings warmth to the person who receives it.

There are thousands of methods of purse-making. Those shown here are typical patterns for typical types. These examples can be modified in size and pattern with your own imagination.

These illustrated patterns are drawn in reduced scale. Cut out these patterns, at least 0.5 cm larger all around than is shown. This will allow for the necessary seams. The faces are always embroidered before the sides are sewn together. Use twill binding or silk ribbon for the trim. Traditional handmade woven braid was commonly used for finishing off the seams, sides, and ends of the purses.

For inner supports, cardboard or interfacing (the interfacing used in dress-making) is suggested. The stiffness of the inner support depends on the type of purse you will be making. The instructions specify which inside backing is needed.

The Heart-Shaped Purse

Materials:
Two pieces 7.5 cm × 16.5 cm face satin
Two pieces 7.5 cm × 16.5 cm interfacing
Two pieces 7.5 cm × 16.5 cm lining
Embroidery threads
One piece 60 cm long thin cord

1. Embroider face satin using seed stitch or satin stitch.
2. Sandwich interfacing between satin face and lining and baste along the top side edges.
3. Fold the pleats (the fan shapes) along the dotted lines as illustrated.
   Start by folding the first pleat up towards you.
5. Repeat this procedure for the other side of the sachet.
6. Stitch the back to the front, right sides together, turn the right side out. Tie thread around the pleats to hold them in place. (Note: fill with incense before securing the pleats).
7. Attach the ends of the cord to the sides of the bag.

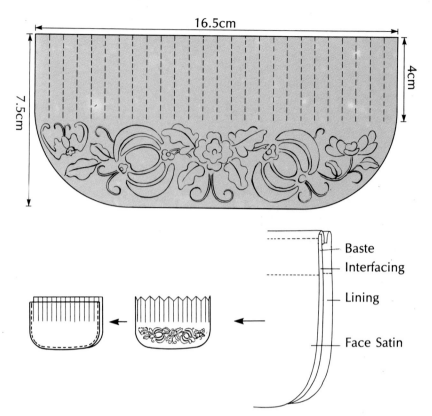

Round Waist Purse

Materials:
One piece 12 cm × 15 cm satin (for face of purse)
One piece 12 cm × 15 cm cardboard backing (for face of purse)
One piece 24 cm × 15 cm lining, fold at the middle
One piece 12 cm × 15 cm fabric for back face
One piece 50 cm long trim
Embroidery threads

1. Embroider the satin face.
2. With 24 cm × 15 cm lining folded in half, (keeping the fold at the bottom of the purse) sandwich the cardboard between the lining and the face satin. Baste all around the outside edges. (The back is also to be basted to the inside lining).
3. Sew on the trim, leaving the top open.
4. Sew on two small pieces of cloth at the sides (see points on diagram) to reinforce and conceal the ends of the trim.

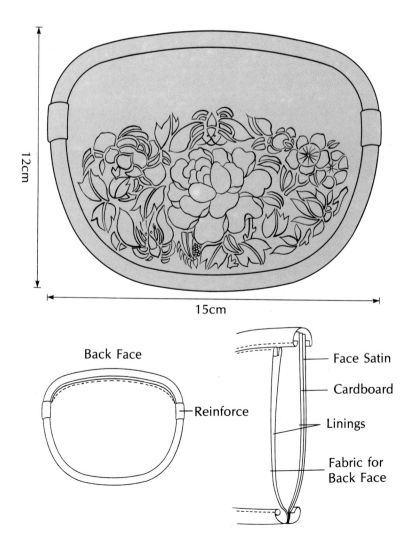

Eye-Glasses Case

Materials:
Two pieces 8 cm × 16 cm face satin
Two pieces 8 cm × 16 cm cardboard paper
Two pieces 8 cm × 16 cm lining
One piece 90 cm long trim
Embroidery threads

1. Embroider both pieces of face satin.
2. Sandwich cardboard between face satin and lining. Stitch together with trim along the sides.
3. Repeat for the other side.
4. Placing the two wrong sides together sew the sides together leaving the top open. Reinforce the two places (on the sides) where the case opens. (See the diagram).
5. Attach the cord to the top of the case for hanging, (optional).

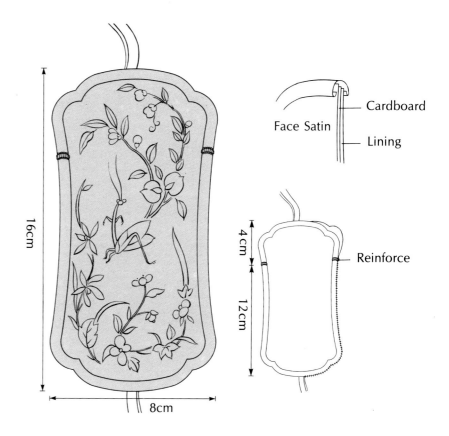

Square Purse I

Materials:
One piece 6 cm × 12 cm face satin
One piece 10.5 cm × 12 cm face satin
One piece 6 cm × 12 cm cardboard
One piece 10.5 cm × 12 cm cardboard
One piece 30 cm × 12 cm lining
One piece 22.5 cm × 12 cm lining
One piece 12 cm × 12 cm fabrie for back face
One piece 70 cm long trim
Embroidery threads

1. Embroider the front face with the satin stitch.
2. Glue the cardboard to the face satin around the outer edges, (forming the rigid front piece and front lid piece).
3. Sew front piece and the back face together, joined by the edging trim.
4. Secure the lid section to the back face with the edging trim as illustrated.
Note: This type of purse can be of single or double face. The above example is for the single face purse. simply attach two front back to back faces if the double face purse is desired.

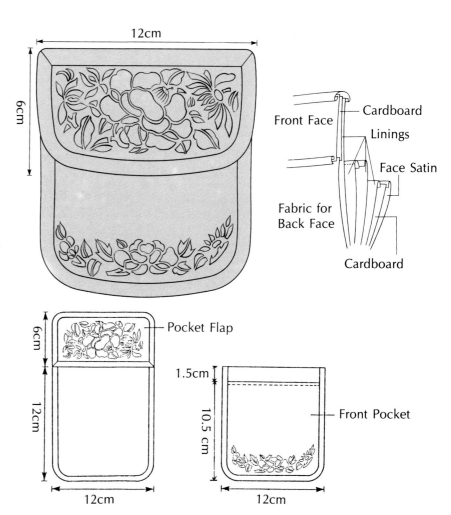

Square Purse II

Materials:
One piece 6 cm × 8.5 cm satin
One piece 8.5 cm × 8.5 cm satin
One piece 6 cm × 8.5 cm cardboard
One piece 8.5 cm × 8.5 cm cardboard
One piece 6 cm × 8.5 cm lining
One piece 8.5 cm × 8.5 cm lining
Two pieces 11.5 cm × 8.5 cm lining (for the pocket)
One piece 30 cm × 7.5 cm plain satin for the backface
One piece 30 cm × 7.5 cm lining
One piece 2 cm × 29 cm side facing
One piece 2 cm × 29 cm lining for the sides
Embriodery threads

1. Embroider the face satin.
2. Prepare the face of the purse as in the example of the Square Purse I.
3. Fold back the 30 cm × 7.5 cm piece of satin. Sew prepared face satin pieces on top of the 11.5 cm × 8.5 cm pocket lining piece. Stitch 2 cm × 29 cm side pieces (face piece with lining) to the front pocket and the folded 30 cm × 7.5 cm pieces of the back pieces.
4. Attach trim along all sewn edges.
5. Attach cord and button to the front face and front flap for closing. (No cord is needed for hanging).

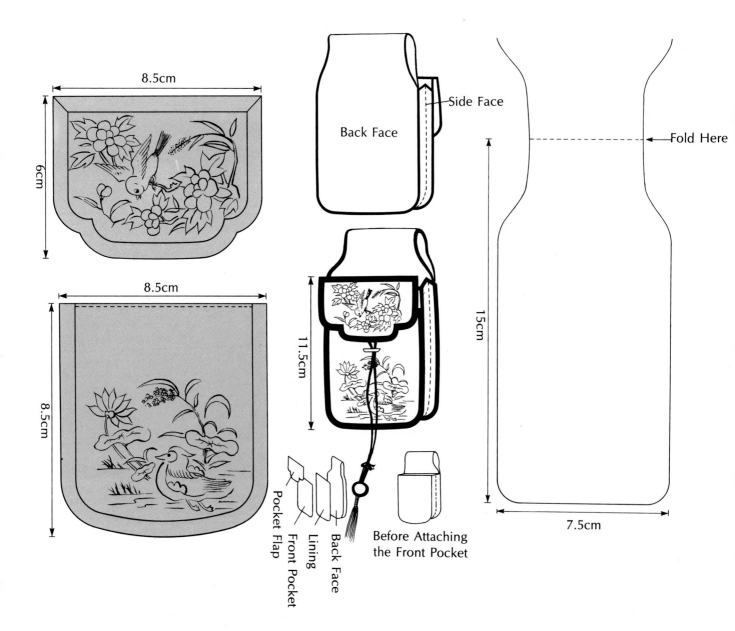

8.5cm

6cm

8.5cm

8.5cm

Back Face

Side Face

11.5cm

Fold Here

15cm

7.5cm

Pocket Flap

Lining

Front Pocket

Back Face

Before Attaching
the Front Pocket

Da-Lien (Money Pocket)

Materials:
Two pieces 7.5 cm × 9 cm satin
Two pieces 7.5 cm × 9 cm cardboard
Two pieces 7.5 cm × 9 cm lining
One piece 18 cm × 27 cm face satin
One piece 18 cm × 27 cm lining
One piece 70 cm long trim
Embroidery threads

1. Embroider the face satins.
2. Sandwich the cardboard between the lining and the front piece and stitch the sides, trim with triming. Set aside.
3. Sew the 18 cm × 25 cm lining together with the 18 cm × 25 cm satin right sides together, leaving the short ends open.
4. Turn right sides out.
5. Fold and stitch 25 cm sides together in center leaving 7.5 cm pouch opening in the middle, finish the 9 cm sides. Buttonhole stitch two ends of the pouch opening several times for reinforcement.
6. Attach the finished 7.5 cm × 9 cm pieces on the ends of each side of the 9 cm × 25 cm piece, leaving the top sides open.

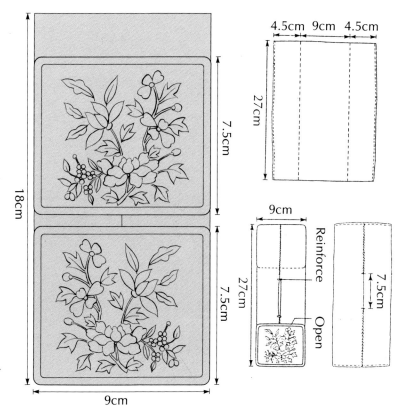

Letter Case

Materials:
Two pieces 9.5 cm × 9 cm face satin
Two pieces 9.5 cm × 9 cm cardboard
Two pieces 9.5 cm × 9 cm lining
One piece 18 cm × 20 cm satin
One piece 18 cm × 20 cm interfacing
One piece 18 cm × 20 cm lining
One piece 140 cm long trim
Embroidery threads

1. Embroider 9.5 cm × 9 cm satin.
2. Sandwich cardboard between face satin and lining, and sew together with side trim. Repeat for other pocket.
3. Baste 18 cm × 20 cm interfacing to wrong side of 18 cm × 20 cm back lining.
4. Sew 20 cm sides together with right side of satin facing the right side of the lining, leaving the short sides open. Turn right sides out.
5. Fold in half the longer sides with the satin on the outside.
6. Blind stitch two open ends together.
7. Sew the trim to the outside edges.
8. Sew on the finished face pieces, leaving the openings at the center.
9. Fold in half.

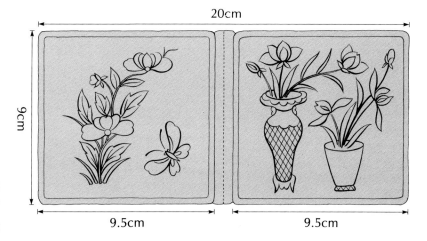

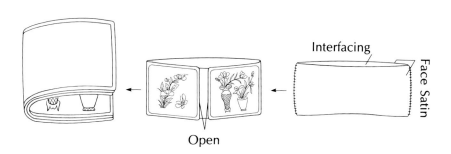

Open

Interfacing

Face Satin